Adapt and Advance

A Faith-Based Step-by-Step Guide to
Turning Trials into Triumphs

Oluwole Babatunde, MD, MPH, PhD

JOIN THE WINNING LAUNCH TEAM FOR THIS BOOK!

Be at the forefront of something truly transformative! By joining the Winning Launch Team, you'll gain early access to the powerful insights in *Adapt and Advance* and play a key role in impacting thousands—perhaps even millions—of lives worldwide.

This is more than just a book launch; it's the beginning of a movement—one that empowers people to turn trials into triumphs and step boldly into their God-given purpose.

Sign up now to be part of the *Adapt and Advance* movement at the link below!

https://oluwolebabatunde.com/launchteam/

AS A THANK YOU FOR PURCHASING AND REVIEWING THE PAPERBACK VERSION, YOU A GET FREE AUDIOBOOK OR E-BOOK

As a token of appreciation for purchasing and reviewing the paperback version of this book, Adapt and Advance, you'll receive a free audiobook or e-book!

Get access by filling out this form

https://oluwolebabatunde.com/review-benefits/

SIGN UP FOR REGULAR FREE PROMO THROUGH AUTHOR NEWSLETTER

To receive information about regular free promotions, sign up for my author newsletter.

https://oluwolebabatunde.com/inform-me/

Praise for *Adapt and Advance*: A Faith-Based Step-
by-Step Guide to Turning Trials into Triumphs
by Oluwole Babatunde, MD, MPH, PhD

The modern landscape of mental health is in need of this book.
With care and expertise, Dr. Babatunde's book does exactly what
his title suggests: it turns trials into triumphs. I am so thankful for
his effort in this work, which is greatly supported by the integrity
with which he leads not only his professional career but even more
so, his personal and family life. The contents of this book are a
trustworthy resource for a hurting world.

Lee McDerment
Lead Pastor of Gatherings, Prayer, and Global Ministries
NewSpring Church, SC, USA.

*Adapt and Advance: A Faith-Based Step-by-Step Guide to
Turning Trials into Triumphs,* **is a must-read for anyone
seeking growth, resilience, and faith-driven success.**
Dr. Wole Babatunde is a remarkable individual of grace, vision,
and unwavering commitment. I had the privilege of meeting
him during my time as Regional Overseer and Pastor of Living
Faith Church, Ilorin, Kwara State, Nigeria, from 2007 to 2009.
Even then, he was a pacesetter and trailblazer among the youth,
demonstrating exceptional leadership and integrity. One of his
notable achievements was his decision to marry the love of his life
despite their shared background as orphans. His deep commitment
to faith and integrity set him apart as a dynamic youth leader. Dr.
Babatunde passionately advanced the kingdom of God, leading
impactful youth initiatives, including hosting life-transforming
gatherings that drew many to Christ. His journey of faith has been
marked by testimonies of God's faithfulness, including the blessing

of twins. Our bond was further strengthened when he and his wife spent their honeymoon in our home, reflecting our admiration for their unwavering dedication to God's work. His book, *Adapt and Advance: A Faith-Based Step-by-Step Guide to Turning Trials into Triumphs*, is a must-read for anyone seeking growth, resilience, and faith-driven success. I highly recommend it as a transformational guide to overcoming life's challenges.

Pastor Joseph Ajibade
Christian Author & Minister
Convener, The Accord of Faith

Adapt and Advance provide readers with a roadmap of how to live a life full or purpose and meaning

I have had the privilege of mentoring Dr. Oluwole Babatunde since the start of his psychiatry residency at PRISMA Health in 2021. Dr. Babatunde has received effusive praise by his peers and patients as a well-rounded scholar who inspires and emboldens individuals to dream without ceasing. Dr. Babatunde places an emphasis on faith, family, and fervor help him flourish personally and professionally. He is the epitome of a physician who recognizes the importance of trusting God irrespective of the seasons one may endure throughout the journey of life. His lived experience of personal loss, resilience, and grit serve as reminders to find the positive aspects in our sufferings. He embodies the principles outlined in his book, *Adapt and Advance* which provide readers with a roadmap of how to live a life full or purpose and meaning. I am thankful for faithful disciples like Dr. Babatunde who continue to spread the gospel of compassion, creativity, and courage.

Frank Clark, MD
Residency Mentor & Attending Psychiatrist, PRISMA Health
Clinical Associate Professor-University of South Carolina School of Medicine-Greenville SC USA

Adapt and Advance is more than a book—it is a roadmap to success, packed with wisdom, faith-driven strategies, and practical insights

Dr. Wole Babatunde is a beacon of faith, resilience, and unwavering character. I have known him for over two decades, and his journey continues to inspire me and many others. His passion for knowledge, discipline, focus, and spirituality is evident in every aspect of his life. No matter the challenge, he adapts and advances, turning obstacles into stepping stones for greater achievements. Knowing him since our school days has reinforced my faith in God, strengthened my belief in myself, and deepened my pursuit of greatness. He is not just a survivor but a relentless motivator—someone who rises above adversity and empowers others to do the same. His life story is a testament to perseverance, divine guidance, and an unshakable commitment to purpose. His book, *Adapt and Advance: A Faith-Based Step-by-Step Guide to Turning Trials into Triumphs*, is a powerful resource for anyone striving to overcome setbacks and turn dreams into reality. It is more than a book—it is a roadmap to success, packed with wisdom, faith-driven strategies, and practical insights. I highly recommend it to anyone determined to rise above challenges and fulfill their God-given destiny.

Pastor Adebayo Akomolafe
Assistant Resident Pastor
Faith Tabernacle, Canaan Land, Ota, Nigeria

I have worked closely with Dr. Oluwole Babatunde since 2014 and have been continually impressed by his intellect, work ethic, kindness, and unwavering commitment to addressing cancer health disparities. As his PhD advisor and ongoing collaborator, I've watched him grow from an exceptional student to a resilient, purpose-driven leader in medicine and research. Wole has authored numerous impactful publications, earned competitive national awards, and consistently demonstrated integrity, creativity, and a passion for service. His journey—marked by faith, perseverance, and productivity—is exactly what Adapt and Advance captures so well. Beyond academia, Wole mentors, volunteers, and uplifts others with a rare blend of humility and vision. He is among the top 1% of students I've ever mentored, and I believe his story will inspire anyone facing life's challenges, just as it has me. This book is a powerful reflection of who he is and what he stands for.

Swann Arp Adams, PhD

Professor, College of Nursing & Department of Epidemiology and Biostatistics University of South Carolina, Columbia, SC, USA.

I have mentored Dr. Oluwole Babatunde since 2016, and I've witnessed his extraordinary growth as a researcher and future leader in cancer health disparities. From the moment I met him, Wole stood out for his intellectual rigor, creativity, and deep passion for improving minority health outcomes. During his postdoctoral fellowship under my mentorship, he led impactful research on geographic and social determinants of cancer disparities and published multiple peer-reviewed manuscripts. Even during the demands of his psychiatry residency, Wole remained remarkably productive—extending his work into psycho-oncology and mental health equity. His ability to turn obstacles into opportunities is a testament to the resilience and insight captured in *Adapt and Advance*. This book reflects not just his academic journey, but the heart of a compassionate and determined physician scientist. I strongly endorse *Adapt and Advance* as an inspiring and practical guide for anyone striving to overcome adversity.

Chanita Hughes Halbert, PhD

Mentor & Professor of Population and Public Health Sciences, University of Southern California, USA

Adapt and advance is not a theory-it is truth lived out - I wholeheartedly recommend this powerful book.

I have known Oluwole since birth--his late mother was a cousin closer than a sister. I was her chief bridesmaid on her wedding day. After high school, Oluwole lived with me and I witnessed firsthand his resilience through life's toughest trials. He became mature earlier than expected, for example, while he was still in the high school, he came home one weekend, his youngest brother who was in fourth grade of elementary school then, lied on his lap and Oluwole was cuddling him like a mother would cuddle her little child. My mother started weeping. Despite the overwhelming odds he faced each phase-college, medical school, and beyond-it was with grace, determination and joy. I fondly called him "happy jolly fellow " because of his unwavering positivity. Adapt and advance is therefore not a theory-it is truth lived out. I wholeheartedly recommend this powerful book.

Hon. Justice Maria Folayan
Retired High Court Judge, Kwara State Judiciary, Ilorin, Nigeria

Some books inspire, some challenge—and then there are books like Adapt and Advance that do both

"Some books inspire, some challenge—and then there are books like this one that do both while making you wonder why you haven't been taking bolder steps all along. Oluwole Babatunde doesn't just talk about resilience and purpose; he lives it. His journey is proof that faith, persistence, and a well-placed journal can turn life's toughest moments into steppingstones.

I've had the privilege of knowing Oluwole personally, and let me tell you—he's the real deal. A man of integrity, wisdom, and relentless faith, he doesn't just write principles; he embodies them. If you're looking for a book that will push you, encourage you, and maybe even convict you a little, this is it.

Garrett Savage
Student Pastor, NewSpring Church, Greenville Campus, SC, USA.

Adapt and Advance is more than inspiration; it reflects a life poured out in quiet strength, persistent faith, and divine purpose
I've known Oluwole Babatunde since he was a baby, and even then, it was clear that God had His hand on his life. After the tragic loss of both his parents, I made it a point to write letters to him while he was still in high school—reminders that he was not forgotten, that he was deeply loved, and that he still had a future worth fighting for.

I also shared something personal with him—something his late father once told me. Oluwole's father had a dream of studying medicine, but life didn't allow it. He hoped that one of his children would one day fulfil that dream. I saw in Oluwole the spark of that dream—and I encouraged him to pursue it.

Today, seeing the man he has become—and now, reading Adapt and Advance—fills my heart with both pride and awe. This book is more than inspiration; it is a reflection of a life poured out in quiet strength, persistent faith, and divine purpose. It is a proof that our past does not define us, but our response to it does.

Oluwole has taken deep pain and turned it into a powerful platform. His journey will move you, stir you, and remind you that even in the darkest moments, God's light still shines. If you have ever needed a push to believe again—this book is your nudge.

Professor Abiodun E O Afolayan, MBBS.
Provost, College of Health Sciences, Al-Hikmah University, Ilorin, Kwara state, Nigeria

Adapt and Advance is not just a title—it's Wole's life in motion and will undoubtedly inspire readers across disciplines.
I am pleased to write an endorsement for Dr. Oluwole Babatunde's book. I have observed Dr. Babatunde as a SAMHSA Minority Fellow, and I can confidently say he embodies what "*Adapt and Advance*" represents. Dr. Babatunde excelled during the fellowship

—particularly with his capstone research project on adverse childhood experiences and mental health disparities,

His ability to translate personal hardship into academic and professional triumph is laudable. *Adapt and Advance* is not just a title—it's Wole's life in motion and will undoubtedly inspire readers across disciplines.

I wholeheartedly recommend this powerful book to anyone navigating personal or professional storms. If you have any questions, please do not hesitate to contact me.

Dr. Regina James
Deputy Medical Director Chief, Division of Diversity and Health Equity American Psychiatric Association Director, SAMHSA Minority Fellowship Program 800 Maine Avenue SW, Suite 900 Washington, DC, USA

Adapt and Advance is a must-read for anyone striving to overcome adversity and live with intention.
As a fellow in the APA's Council on Research and Health Disparities, Dr. Oluwole Babatunde stood out for his tenacity, insight, and trailblazing research. His work exploring the intersection of adverse childhood experiences, race, and mental health—especially in older adults and cancer survivors—pushed critical conversations forward in ways few young investigators have. *Adapt and Advance reflects his unique journey: rising through loss, cultural transitions, and rigorous training to emerge as a voice of healing and hope. Wole writes with the same passion and precision he brings to his research, making this book both accessible and impactful. What's remarkable is not just what he's achieved, but how—through faith, grit, and service to others. I've watched him grow into a leader who truly embodies resilience, and this book offers that gift to every reader. Adapt and Advance is a must-read for anyone striving to overcome adversity and live with intention.*

Dr. Diana E. Clarke
Director, Division of Research and Health Disparities American Psychiatric Association Washington DC, USA.

**If you're looking for real hope, practical wisdom, and the
spark to keep going, Adapt and Advance will speak to you**
Oluwole Babatunde and I were classmates in medical school, and
even then, his passion for purpose was undeniable. He poured his
heart into writing—birthing his first mini book, Becoming Great, in
2002. Watching that little book sell over 1,000 copies in a year was
inspiring, but even more powerful was the vision and fire behind it.

Oluwole didn't just write to impress—he wrote to impact. And over
two decades later, that same passion has matured into something
deeper, richer, and even more life-giving. Adapt and Advance isn't
just another motivational book—it's a living testament of grit,
grace, and godly resilience.

Having witnessed his journey firsthand, I can say Oluwole has
always been intentional about rising above life's limitations. From
personal loss to professional growth, he's never let pain have the
final word. This book is the overflow of that journey—a call to
anyone who feels stuck, weary, or unsure of what's next.

If you're looking for real hope, practical wisdom, and the spark
to keep going, Adapt and Advance will speak to you—just like
Oluwole's words have spoken to many since that first book in 2002.

Dr. Tayo Onaleye, MBBS.
Classmate, College of Health Sciences, University of Ilorin
Pastor of NEXT LEVEL CHRISTIAN CENTER, Lagos, Nigeria.

**Adapt and Advance is a profound reflection of Wole's journey,
anchored in purpose, perseverance, and service to humanity.**
I have had the privilege of working closely with Dr. Oluwole
Babatunde during his psychiatry residency. Over the years, he
has exemplified unwavering dedication, remarkable intellectual
depth, and an extraordinary commitment to serving others. Wole's
trajectory—from earning a PhD in public health to becoming the

esteemed Administrative Chief Resident—stands as a testament to his resilience, visionary leadership, and unparalleled academic achievements. His distinguished body of work encompasses over 65 peer-reviewed publications, impactful national research presentations, and the prestigious NIH F99/K00 award, which highlights his innovative contributions to the field. Yet, what truly defines Wole is his heart. His boundless empathy, unrelenting passion for addressing health disparities, and ability to uplift those around him with his radiant positivity and steadfast determination make him a force for good in every sense. His life's philosophy—Adapt and Advance—is a profound reflection of his journey, anchored in purpose, perseverance, and service to humanity. I wholeheartedly recommend this inspiring work to anyone seeking a beacon of hope and guidance through life's most challenging seasons.

Dr. Anusuiya Nagar, MD.
Clinical Assistant Professor University of South Carolina School of Medicine Greenville Program Director, Greer Psychiatry Residency Program Department of Psychiatry Prisma Health – Upstate, SC, USA.

l strongly recommend Adapt and Advance to all high school, college and university students seeking hope, direction and the courage to keep going.
As an educator and former Deputy Rector at Kwara State Polytechnic, l encountered many students who faced adversity- but the resilience l witnessed in Oluwole was truly exceptional. Humble, consistent and full of life, he stood out not just academically but in character. Adapt and Advance is a powerful reflection of his journey and mindset. It is an inspiring guide for anyone navigating life's challenges. l strongly recommend this book to all high school, college and university students seeking hope, direction and the courage to keep going.

Mrs O.O Ajibade
Former Deputy Rector Kwara State Polytechnic, Ilorin, Kwara State, Nigeria.

Adapt and Advance reflects not just his story, but a message of hope and transformation for anyone seeking to rise above life's trials

I have known Dr. Oluwole Babatunde since he arrived in the United States in 2014. From the beginning, he has exemplified the very spirit of Adapt and Advance—a powerful blend of resilience, faith, and purpose. Wole is an embodiment of hard work and determination, consistently pushing through challenges with grace and grit. His journey is both humbling and inspiring. This book reflects not just his story, but a message of hope and transformation for anyone seeking to rise above life's trials. I highly recommend Adapt and Advance to readers everywhere.

Dr. Oluwole Ariyo, PhD.
Dean of Mathematics and Natural Sciences
Associate Professor of Biology, Allen University, Columbia, SC, USA

Adapt and Advance is not just a book; it's a living message of hope, courage, and divine resilience

Oluwole's dad was my senior in the equivalent of high school in the 1970s. In the early 1990s, we jointly owned Abaso Hospital. Oluwole had lost his mum when I first met him. Later, his dad passed away when he was thirteen years old. The incident never deterred Oluwole; he did not allow this to define him. I fondly remember his tenacity and quietness—but with a great sense of responsibility, pursuing his career and with serious commitment to the faith. Oluwole had no moment for regrets or sorrow. He was humble, easy to please, and undemanding. I witnessed Oluwole face life's harshest realities at a tender age—yet he chose faith over fear and purpose over despair. *Adapt and Advance* is a moving testament to that journey. It's not just a book; it's a living message of hope, courage, and divine resilience. Oluwole writes with authenticity, shaped by trials and triumphs. This book will inspire anyone facing adversity to rise, rebuild, and rediscover purpose.

Pastor (Dr.) Olayinka Oladosu, MBBS.

Health Compliance Manager, Moreno Valley, California, USA

If you've ever felt like giving up, Adapt and Advance will give you a reason to rise again.

I watched Oluwole grow up after the heartbreaking loss of both parents at such a young age. I saw the tears, the quiet battles, the lonely seasons—but I also saw the unwavering determination, the faith that refused to die, and the courage that kept him moving forward.

As the first child of his parents, I am thrilled for becoming the father of his younger siblings at a very tender age.

This book is not just a message—it's a mantle. It carries the weight of a journey that proves pain can produce purpose, and that brokenness can birth brilliance.

Oluwole doesn't just talk about rising above challenges—he's a living example of it. A young man of integrity, humility, and deep conviction, his life is a testament to what God can do with a surrendered heart.

If you've ever felt like giving up, Adapt and Advance will give you a reason to rise again. Let this book remind you that your story isn't over—and your future is still full of hope.

Sam Aweda

Jesus for the World Revival Mission (Peoples' Church), Ilorin, Kwara state, Nigeria.

XVI ADAPT AND ADVANCE

Adapt and Advance is more than just words on pages—it's a reflection of Oluwole's life, poured out in raw, real, and redemptive honesty

I've had the privilege of knowing Wole and his wife for over a decade through NewSpring Church in Columbia, SC. They are truly incredible people with a deep love for God and others. I've witnessed Wole faithfully serving our youth through Fuse (our youth ministry) with unwavering integrity. Now, God has graced him with the opportunity to publish his first book, Adapt and Advance. This book is more than just words on pages—it's a reflection of Oluwole's life, poured out in raw, real, and redemptive honesty. If you're seeking hope and direction, this book will challenge and inspire you in powerful ways.

Roy S. Rogers
Author of The Making of a Good Man, Columbia SC USA

Adapt and Advance is not just a book—it's a powerful testimony of grace, grit, and godly wisdom

I'm really grateful to God for where I am today and also for the great people He has used to influence me positively of which Dr Wole Babatunde readily comes to mind.

I had the privilege of walking closely with Dr Oluwole Babatunde during his years in medical school (23 years ago and the relationship has been blossoming) and one thing was always clear—this is a man of unshakable resilience and unwavering faith. In the face of adversity, he chose purpose over pity, action over despair, he is a goal-getter.

He's always been a pure source of inspiration and I'm so grateful to God that our path crossed in life when it mattered most. When I wrote my first book in 2007, I couldn't but acknowledge him as a crucial part of my journey. Adapt and Advance is not just a book— it's a powerful testimony of grace, grit, and godly wisdom.

Dr Oluwole writes from the trenches of real life, not from the sidelines. His story will stir your spirit and challenge you to embrace your own God-given journey with boldness and hope.

Akinola Akinyemi
Author - Leadership Vacancy,
President Heritage Leadership Academy and
Senior Pastor, God's Heritage Christian Centre, Lagos, Nigeria

Adapt and Advance is a must-read for every young man and woman seeking practical wisdom on navigating life's challenges with resilience and faith

I have known Oluwole since our days in medical school, and he has always stood out as a committed, consistent, and purpose-driven individual. Through many trials, he has continued to adapt and advance with unwavering determination and grace. His story is both inspiring and instructive. Adapt and Advance is a must-read for every young man and woman seeking practical wisdom on navigating life's challenges with resilience and faith. I strongly recommend this book.

Dr. John Agboola, MD.
Physician, NY, USA
Author of "Why Am I Here? How did I get here? Where am I going?"

I had the privilege of being Oluwole Babatunde's classmate in medical school, and his journey has always inspired me.

He faced deep personal loss and significant challenges, yet rose with uncommon resilience, unwavering focus, and faith that never wavered. Oluwole distinguished himself—not just through academic excellence, but through his strength of character and heart for others.

Adapt and Advance is a moving reflection of his journey—raw, faith-filled, and deeply insightful. If you've ever doubted your ability to rise again, this book will remind you that your trials can become tools for transformation.

Dr. Yetunde Ayo Oyalowo
Director, Market Women Health Initiative, Lagos, Nigeria

Adapt and Advance is more than a book—it's Oluwole's lived journey of turning pain into purpose
I've known Oluwole Babatunde all his life—not just as a cousin, but as someone I've admired deeply. I watched him navigate the painful loss of both parents at such a young age, yet he never lost his faith, resilience, or drive. *Adapt and Advance* is more than a book—it's Oluwole's lived journey of turning pain into purpose. Every page reflects his strength, honesty, and unshakable belief in God's plan. If you've ever faced hardship and wondered if you could rise again, this book will remind you that with faith and focus, triumph is possible.

Funmi Abioye (née Babatunde)
Registered Nurse, Oklahoma, USA
Cousin & Lifelong Witness to the Journey

I've walked closely with Oluwole Babatunde—first as a classmate, then as a housemate and neighbor during our final years in medical school and housemanship.
His character stood out consistently: dependable, purpose-driven, and unwavering in faith and integrity. *Adapt and Advance* isn't just another motivational book—it's a deeply personal roadmap shaped by real struggles and courageous choices. Oluwole doesn't speak from theory; he writes from lived experience. His journey

will stir your heart, spark your faith, and push you toward your own breakthrough. If you're ready to rise above life's trials, this book will guide you there.

Dr. Anthony Joseph
Classmate & Friend, University of Ilorin College of Health Sciences
Consultant Family Physician, Department of Family Medicine, Sobi Specialist Hospital, Ilorin, Kwara state, Nigeria.

Adapt and Advance is a blueprint for turning life's setbacks into launching pads.
As Wole's younger brother, I've had the privilege of witnessing his unwavering commitment to faith, growth, and resilience. Adapt and Advance is not just theory—it's his real life story of rising through adversity with intentionality and grace. This book equips readers with timeless strategies and spiritual truths to face life's fiercest storms. As an author and entrepreneur, I found its lessons applicable not just personally but professionally. If you're ready to stop reacting to life and start building your God-given destiny, this is your guide. Read it. Live it. Advance.

Dr. Akinola Babatunde
Author of Establish Your Empire,
Chancellor at PATRAL Multiversity,
Professor of Electrical and Electronics Engineering at Western Technical College, Lacrosse WI, USA

Adapt and Advance: A Faith-Based Step-by-Step Guide to Turning Trials into Triumphs
Copyright ©2025 by Oluwole Babatunde, Md, MPH, Phd.

All Rights Reserved
No part of this publication may be reproduced, transmitted, or stored in any form—whether mechanical or electronic, including photocopying, recording, or any information storage system—without prior written permission from the author or publisher, except for brief quotations in reviews.

DISCLAIMER:
The advice and strategies contained herein may not be suitable for every situation. This work is published with the understanding that neither the author nor the publisher is engaged in providing medical, legal, accounting, or any other professional services.

The author and publisher disclaim any liability for damages arising from the use of this material. References to organizations or websites in this work are for citation or informational purposes only. Their inclusion does not imply endorsement of the content or recommendations provided by these entities. Readers are advised that the information or recommendations on referenced websites may have changed or become outdated since the publication of this work.

ISBN: 979-8-89694-284-9 - eBook
ISBN: 979-8-89694-285-6 - Paperback
ISBN: 979-8-89694-286-3 - Hardcover
ISBN: 979-8-89694-357-0 - Audiobook

DEDICATION

My parents:

This book is lovingly dedicated to the memory of Solomon A. Babatunde, my late father, an extraordinary man who taught me life's fundamental principles during the 13 precious years we had together. It is also dedicated to the memory of my late mother, Esther Omonike Babatunde, whose ever-smiling presence and unwavering love enriched my life during the seven precious years we shared together before she transitioned to glory. I miss both of you deeply and hold onto the hope that we will one day reunite at the feet of Jesus, where we will worship together eternally.

While I cannot name everyone who stepped in to fill the role of parent after the loss of both my mother and father, I want to express my deepest gratitude to Honorable Justice Maria Folayan and the late Pa Israel Babatunde. Your love, guidance, and unwavering support meant the world to me—Honorable Justice Maria Folayan, for being a mother figure, and the late Pa Israel Babatunde, for standing as a father in my journey. Your impact on my life is immeasurable, and I am forever grateful. To everyone who stood in the gap and supported me—emotionally, financially, spiritually, physically, and in every other way—I am deeply grateful. It truly takes a village to raise and uplift a person, and I'm thankful for each of you.

My wife:

I also dedicate this book to the love of my life, my wife, Bukky Babatunde. You have been my greatest gift, my unwavering supporter, and my source of so much joy and laughter. You challenge my perspectives, stretch my vision of what is possible, and remind me that our differences make us stronger. They say opposites attract, and that could not be truer for us. Though we often see things differently, our unique outlooks enrich our union, making us better together. You are not just my better half—you are the best thing that has ever happened to me. As I always say, you are my greatest gift. Every single day, you help me see life differently, keep things in perspective, and find balance. I love you endlessly, and I am forever grateful for you.

My children:

Lastly, I dedicate this book to my children, my twin boys, Temilola and Teniola. You have been a part of my dreams since the day you were born. Your arrival changed everything, igniting a fire within me to be the best father I can be and to pursue my purpose with unwavering passion. Knowing that you look up to me pushes me to be the best version of myself at all times. I am incredibly proud of the young individuals you are becoming, and I have no doubt your future is filled with greatness. I continue to work hard to make you proud, just as you inspire me daily by striving for excellence. Thank you for all the ways you have contributed to making this book a reality—your support means more than words can express.

A MESSAGE TO MY READERS

This book is for everyone, regardless of faith or beliefs. While I'm a Christian and my faith deeply shapes my life, the principles in this book are universal. They are applicable to anyone seeking resilience, purpose, and progress. My aim is not to alienate non-Christian readers but to invite everyone to learn from the insights I've gained through experience and faith.

I could have written this book without referencing Christianity or Bible verses, but doing so would be betraying myself, as Christianity has influenced my approach to life's challenges more than anything else. However, I encourage you, regardless of your faith, to read this book with an open mind, take what resonates with you, and leave what doesn't. My hope is that the principles shared here will inspire and empower you.

If you have feedback or questions, please feel free to contact me at: wole@oluwolebabatunde.com. I'm also working on future books that have a broader, non-faith-based perspective, so keep an eye out for those. Thank you for taking this journey with me.

CONTENTS

INTRODUCTION

My Journey with Adapt and Advance

In 2002, during my fifth year of medical school in Nigeria, I published what I consider my pre-first book, titled *Becoming Great*. Using a local printer, my friend and colleague helped me produce 1,000 copies, which sold out the same year. While the book didn't have a wide reach or even an ISBN, it marked the beginning of my journey as a writer. That experience ignited a desire to write books that help people navigate difficult times.

Since then, my journey has been anything but straightforward. After graduating from medical school in 2003, I completed my internship in 2004 and served in the National Youth Service Corps (NYSC) in 2006. During this period, I worked briefly in private hospitals before joining a government hospital in Kaiama, Kwara State. In 2007, I began my residency in community medicine/public health, which I completed in 2011. For three years, I worked as a consultant in community health before moving to the United States to pursue a PhD. I completed my doctorate in 2019, followed by a two-year postdoctoral fellowship. I am currently completing my psychiatry residency, which will conclude in 2025.

Those years of constant transitions made it challenging to focus on writing. I often joke that I've been in school my entire life—except for the few years before kindergarten and my time as a practicing physician in Nigeria. However, on July 1, 2024, I decided to dedicate myself to this book, which reflects principles I've used to overcome challenges, adapt, and advance through life's trials.

A Life Marked by Loss: My Father's Death

In December 1991, I was a happy tenth-grade boarding school student in Ilorin, Nigeria. My father, a pharmacist, frequently visited me when he came to town to purchase supplies for his pharmacy. On one such trip, my friends and I happened to see him by chance. We greeted him, joked about how I had grown taller than him, and he gave us some money before parting ways—both of us clueless about how much of a twist our lives were about to take.

The next morning, December 3, 1991, I was called to the vice principal's office, where I was asked to return home. Immediately upon arrival, I was met with the devastating news: my father had been killed in a car accident. It felt like my reality had been torn apart, leaving me standing in the ruins of the life I once knew.

My mother had died six years earlier, heavily pregnant, and my father had been my anchor ever since—and now he was gone too. At just 13, the weight of my unknown future pressed down on me, and I had no idea how I would bear it—where to turn, or who to turn to.

My father had always been a man of ambition and positivity. He was the first in our family to attend graduate school, and ran his own pharmacy. Despite our middle-class lifestyle, he instilled in me the values of hard work and resilience. His sudden death left me technically homeless, moving from one relative's home to another, but his legacy of perseverance stayed with me.

Finding My Strength: Overcoming Adversity

After losing both parents, life became a series of hard knocks. It was as if the world was determined to test how much I could endure. Yet, I managed to complete high school, advanced-level studies, and gain admission into medical school in Nigeria. Medical school was a six-year program split into preclinical and clinical phases. While I excelled in the preclinical years, my fourth year—marked by pathology and pharmacology exams—was a tough nut to crack. I began failing exams, which jeopardized my academic progress and future as a doctor.

Desperate and overwhelmed, I turned to my Christian faith for guidance. I sought spiritual mentorship and joined a church founded by Bishop David Oyedepo. This period reignited my faith and discipline. I began reading one motivational book per week, diving into works by authors like Myles Munroe, Mike Murdock, and Rick Warren. These books, coupled with my spiritual journey, helped me realign my focus and overcome academic struggles.

Adapting and Advancing

The principles I share in this book have been born out of my life experiences—many of them rooted in desperation. They reflect lessons I've learned from books, mentors, and personal reflection. However, your journey is your journey alone, and mine is mine. As you read, I encourage you to take what works for you and adapt it to fit your circumstances. Some ideas may not resonate, and that's okay. What matters is that you keep moving forward, learning, and growing.

In this book, I will be utilizing the concept of MAP-LAMP as a guiding framework to convey my points effectively. The acronym MAP-LAMP represents the seven key sections that form the foundation of this approach: **M** for Meaning-Making, **A** for Act, **P** for Plan, **L** for Learn, **A** for Alliance Formation, **M** for Mission Focus, and **P** for Pray. Each section is designed to provide practical insights and strategies for navigating challenges, fostering growth, and achieving a purposeful, fulfilling life.

Thank you for taking the time to read this book. I hope it inspires you to face your challenges with courage, adapt to life's changes, and advance toward your goals. Together, let's embark on this journey of growth and resilience.

SECTION 1

MEANING MAKING

This section describes how to navigate life's challenges by finding meaning, defining purpose, and building resilience. The following chapters, encompassing seven powerful principles, will help you discover the strength to move forward, even through life's deepest trials. By embracing these strategies, you will learn to transform obstacles into opportunities for growth, develop a lasting sense of purpose, and build resilience that allows you to thrive in any circumstance.

In Chapter 1, we will explore how to find meaning and purpose in each difficult life experience. Understanding that every challenge offers a lesson will help you learn to frame your hardships as opportunities for growth. This foundational chapter will set the stage for how you can align your daily actions with a greater purpose, using even the most painful moments to build strength.

Moving into Chapter 2, you will discover how to define your "why"—the purpose that fuels both your long-term and short-term goals. Identifying what drives you enables resilience in the face of adversity, offering the clarity you need to focus your energy on what truly matters.

Building on that foundation, Chapter 3 will teach you how to turn your mess into your message. Every failure, loss, and obstacle can be reframed into a powerful story of resilience and hope, offering comfort to others walking a similar path. This mindset helps transform your challenges into stepping stones, leading to both personal and collective healing.

As we progress into Chapter 4, we'll dive into the critical role of failure in your journey. Embracing setbacks as part of the process, you will learn to see each misstep not as an end, but as a lesson that propels you forward.

In Chapter 5, you will be reminded that no matter where you've come from, what matters most is where you're going. Your past does not define you; it's your vision for the future that shapes your reality. Through focused actions, you'll develop the mindset necessary to rise above limitations.

As we move into Chapter 6, you will explore how to navigate life's "deep waters"—those overwhelming seasons of adversity. With the power of faith and resilience, you will learn practical strategies to keep going even when the tide seems too strong.

Finally, in Chapter 7, we will examine how journaling can serve as a powerful tool to adapt and advance through life's challenges. Writing down your reflections, lessons, and emotions provides clarity, helps track growth, and builds a lasting sense of gratitude and faith, reinforcing resilience with every written word.

CHAPTER 1

Finding Meaning and Purpose in Each Difficult Life Experience

Why do some people thrive in hardship while others struggle? The answer often lies in their sense of purpose. Understanding this difference can be life-changing, as a strong sense of purpose shapes how we navigate challenges. This fundamental difference influences how people respond to difficulties, shaping their ability to overcome obstacles and find fulfillment.

In this chapter, you will learn how to find meaning and purpose even in life's most challenging moments. We'll explore how purpose can transform adversity into opportunities for growth and highlight practical steps to help you live with intention every day. By discovering meaning in your experiences, you'll build resilience and create a life aligned with your unique calling.

Finding meaning in hardship can be the key to resilience, allowing individuals to turn struggles into stepping stones for growth. Throughout history, great minds have recognized the power of purpose in overcoming adversity, as reflected in Viktor Frankl's words:

> "Life is never made unbearable by circumstances,
> but only by lack of meaning and purpose."
>
> —Viktor Frankl

Frankl's insights reflect a timeless truth—purpose has the power to sustain us through even the darkest moments. Many successful individuals have also drawn strength from a deep sense of meaning, using it to overcome adversity and achieve greatness.

How This Worked For Others

In his book *Man's Search for Meaning*, Viktor Frankl recounts how he survived unimaginable suffering in Nazi concentration camps. He attributed his endurance to the power of meaning and purpose. Despite the horrors, he found purpose in envisioning a future beyond the camps and focusing on the greater good he could achieve.

My Story

Like Frankl, I also had to search for meaning and purpose after facing one of the most painful moments of my life. Finding purpose in suffering is never easy, but it can shape the way we move forward, just as it did for him. Similarly, I had to navigate profound loss at a young age, and in doing so, I discovered the strength that comes from embracing meaning even in the face of deep sorrow.

I still vividly remember December 3, 1991—a day that shattered my world and changed my life forever. I remember being called to the vice principal's office at my high school's boarding house in Ilorin, Nigeria. He was a close friend of my father and had always been a source of guidance and encouragement. But that day, there was a heaviness in his voice, an unspoken sorrow that made my heart pound. I remember being escorted to my uncle's home, where I saw a gathering of somber faces, their hushed whispers filling me with an unbearable dread. My uncle had sat me down, his eyes filled with pain, and gently told me about my father's death.

The words didn't make sense at first. I didn't want them to make sense. I had seen him the previous day when he came for one of his trips to purchase medications in Ilorin. We had shared jokes. And now, I was being told that he never made it back home alive. I kept replaying that last interaction with my father in my mind, clinging to it as if somehow it could bring him back to me.

This devastating loss only deepened the pain I had already carried since losing my mother at the age of six. It felt cruel, as if life had taken too much from me too soon. I remember sitting in that room, surrounded by grieving relatives, feeling as if I had been swallowed by a hollow, inescapable silence. My young mind wrestled with the painful question: "Why? Why did both of my parents have to be taken from me?"

The weight of that grief threatened to crush me, but even in the depths of sorrow, something inside me refused to let despair have the final word.

Through my tears, I made a silent vow—this tragedy would not define me. I would not allow grief to steal the future my parents had dreamed for me. I decided to rise above the pain, to find meaning in their memory, and to live a life that honored their sacrifice. Their absence fueled me, pushing me forward when giving up felt like the easier option.

Adapt and Advance

To adapt means to accept change and adjust to the new realities of your challenges. To advance means to take proactive steps toward growth, notwithstanding what happened. In my case, while grappling with the loss of my parents, I discovered that finding meaning and purpose was a daily effort. I realized that life's challenges could either break us or build us. I chose to let them build me.

One driving purpose emerged from my father's dream for one of his children to become a medical doctor. Though I already had a passion for medicine, this vision gave me an additional sense of purpose that propelled me forward despite many obstacles.

Lesson or Explanation of Quotes

Finding meaning and purpose in difficult situations isn't just about overcoming hardship; it's about transforming that hardship into a stepping stone for growth. As John D. Rockefeller said, "Singleness of purpose is one of the chief essentials for success in life." When we find meaning, our struggles become fuel for resilience, creativity, and progress.

In *Man's Search for Meaning*, Viktor Frankl outlines three primary ways to find meaning and purpose in difficult life experiences. Drawing from his profound observations during his time in Nazi concentration camps, Frankl's ideas emphasize the human capacity to find meaning even in the most challenging circumstances. Below are the three main ways he identifies:

Three Primary Ways to Find Meaning and Purpose In Difficult Life Experiences

1. By Creating or Accomplishing Something

Frankl suggests that engaging in meaningful work or pursuing creative endeavors allows individuals to find purpose, even in the face of adversity. When we dedicate ourselves to producing something valuable—whether it be art, a professional goal, or contributing to others' well-being—we transcend our suffering by focusing on something greater than ourselves.

In Frankl's book, he shared that even in the harsh conditions of the concentration camps, prisoners who took on responsibilities, such as comforting others or imagining work they wanted to complete after liberation, found their lives imbued with purpose.

In the modern context, someone facing a difficult situation can create meaning by setting goals, pursuing passions, or contributing to projects that impact others positively. Imagine a woman who lost her job during a recession, and instead of wallowing in sadness, she started a nonprofit to help others in the same situation. By creating something valuable, she transformed her hardship into purpose

Like Frankl, since my university days, I have wholeheartedly shared my journey of losing both parents at a young age, using my story to uplift and inspire others—especially in life's most challenging moments. Rather than allowing pain to define me, I have embraced it as a platform to strengthen those around me, reminding them that resilience can emerge even from life's deepest losses.

From 2000 to 2007, while leading the house cell fellowship for Living Faith Church, I used my experiences to encourage others in their faith, showing them that God's grace is ever-present, even in times of hardship. Between 2003 and 2007, I hosted monthly success seminars for young people, pouring into their aspirations and reminding them that setbacks are not the end, but stepping stones to greatness. Since 2015, I have led Fuse groups for high school students at Newspring Church, mentoring and guiding them through their own struggles, helping them see that even in brokenness, purpose can be found.

Through every opportunity, I have remained committed to sharing my story—not as a tale of tragedy, but as a testament to the power of faith, resilience, and perseverance. I stand as living proof that trials, no matter how overwhelming, can be transformed into triumphs.

2. By Experiencing or Encountering Someone or Something

Frankl emphasizes that meaning can be found through love, relationships, and appreciation of beauty or nature. The experience of love—be it for a person, idea, or cause—gives life profound significance. Similarly, encounters with the beauty of art, music, or nature can inspire and uplift the human spirit.

During his time in the camps, Frankl often drew strength from memories of his wife and the love he felt for her, despite their physical separation. Difficult situations can be navigated by cherishing meaningful relationships, expressing love, or immersing oneself in experiences that inspire awe, like admiring art, reading literature, or connecting with nature.

3. By Adopting an Attitude Toward Suffering

Frankl's most revolutionary idea is that even suffering can have meaning when it is approached with the right mindset. While suffering itself is not inherently meaningful, our response to it can be. By embracing suffering as an opportunity to grow, learn, or demonstrate resilience, we can find purpose even in pain.

Frankl observed how some prisoners maintained dignity and inner freedom despite extreme suffering, choosing to find meaning in their suffering by viewing it as a test of their character. In challenging times, individuals can adopt a mindset that frames suffering as a pathway to growth. This might include seeing hardship as a way to develop resilience, find spiritual growth, or contribute to others through one's story or example.

Frankl's three pathways to meaning—creating, experiencing love or beauty, and transforming suffering—offer a profound framework for navigating life's difficulties. These approaches demonstrate that no matter the circumstances, meaning is always within reach, as long as we engage with life purposefully and with an open heart.

Serving as a home cell leader in Living Faith Church, Ilorin, from 2000 to 2010 was a powerful application of these principles in my life. Through my leadership role, I actively contributed to the spiritual growth of individuals and the expansion of the church, both locally and internationally.

This aligned with Frankl's first pathway—creating or accomplishing something meaningful. Despite facing my own challenges, I dedicated myself to guiding others, fostering a strong faith community, and supporting members in their personal and spiritual development. In doing so, I found fulfillment beyond my struggles, proving that even in difficult seasons, we can transcend our pain by building something greater than ourselves.

My time at the church also exemplified the second pathway— experiencing meaning through love, relationships, and encounters with beauty. Worship, with its deep integration of music and art, became a source of healing and inspiration for me. Singing and dancing in services uplifted my spirit and provided solace in tough seasons. This experience reinforced my belief in the power of beauty to restore the soul. Additionally, I embraced suffering as an opportunity for growth, embodying Frankl's third pathway. Instead of allowing hardships to define me, I saw them as lessons, constantly reading books about successful people and pursuing formal education to equip myself for the future.

By transforming pain into purpose, I developed resilience and a deeper sense of mission, ultimately shaping the person I am today.

Finding Meaning From The Bible.

The Bible offers profound guidance on finding meaning and purpose in difficulties, emphasizing faith, trust in God, and eternal hope. Personally, that is where I find the most meaning. Scripture reminds us that trials can refine and strengthen us, shaping our character and drawing us closer to God. James 1:2-4 encourages believers to "count it all joy" when facing trials, as they produce perseverance and maturity. Similarly, Romans 8:28 reassures us that "all things work together for good" for those who love God.

In hardships, we find purpose by serving others, as Jesus exemplified through His sacrificial love (John 13:34). The Psalms, particularly Psalm 23, remind us of God's presence and comfort in dark times. Additionally, 2 Corinthians 1:4 calls us to use our experiences to comfort others.

Ultimately, the Bible teaches that suffering is temporary, pointing to eternal hope in Christ (2 Corinthians 4:17), where ultimate meaning and purpose are fulfilled.

Bible Verses and Explanations

1. Jeremiah 1:5

"Before I formed you in the womb I knew you [and approved of you as My chosen instrument], and before you were born I consecrated you [to Myself as My own]; I have appointed you as a prophet to the nations."

This verse reminds us that God has a specific plan and purpose for every life, even before birth. No matter how difficult our circumstances, His purpose for us remains steadfast.

2. Romans 8:28

"And we know [with great confidence] that God [who is deeply concerned about us] causes all things to work together [as a plan] for good for those who love God, to those who are called according to His plan and purpose."

Even when life feels chaotic, this verse assures us that God can bring good out of every situation, aligning it with His greater plan for our lives.

Very Important Next Step

Take time to reflect on a challenging experience in your life and ask yourself what lessons it taught you and how it can shape your purpose. Daily reflection helps uncover the unique talents and passions God has placed within you, and allows you to view challenges as opportunities for growth. Consider how you can use today's struggles to contribute meaningfully to others, and write down one action you will take this week to align your life more closely with your purpose. By reframing hardships as opportunities, you transform suffering into strength, gaining clarity and resilience. Set aside quiet time for journaling, focusing on the emotional and practical impact of your experiences, and revisit these reflections to refine your purpose over time.

Worksheet or Exercise for Growth

1. Reflect on a difficult experience you've faced. Write down:

- What happened?
- What lesson did it teach you?
- How can you use that lesson to help others or fulfill your purpose?

2. Identify one passion or skill you've been neglecting. Plan one small step to reignite it this week.

- Remember that meaning and purpose evolve with time and experiences.
- Purposeful living requires intentionality; keep revisiting and refining your goals.
- If you struggle to find meaning, lean on faith, trusted mentors, or supportive communities.

Finding meaning and purpose is not a one-time event; it's a continuous journey. As you navigate life's challenges, remember that purpose gives direction and transforms adversity into opportunities for growth. In the next chapter, we'll explore the power of perseverance and how to stay steadfast in your purpose when the road gets tough.

CHAPTER 2

Discover Your "Why": Long-Term and Short-Term

Why do people with a strong purpose never get lost? Simple. Because they always have a 'why' to guide them.

A clear sense of purpose acts as an internal compass, keeping us on track even in the face of uncertainty. By understanding your "why," you can navigate life's challenges with confidence and direction, ensuring every step aligns with your greater goals.

In this chapter, you will discover the importance of identifying your "why"—both for the long term and the short term. Understanding your purpose gives you the strength to endure challenges, adapt, and thrive. Whether it's a major life goal or daily priorities, defining your "why" helps you stay focused, resilient, and fulfilled.

Having a clear purpose not only provides direction but also builds resilience, allowing us to persevere through life's toughest moments. History and philosophy have long emphasized the power of purpose, as reflected in Viktor Frankl's profound words: "He who has a reason to live can bear almost any how."

Frankl's insight reveals a timeless truth—when we anchor ourselves to a strong purpose, we can withstand even the harshest trials. His own life serves as a powerful example of how embracing a "why" can transform suffering into strength.

How This Worked For Successful People: Howard Thurman, Victor Frankl

Howard Thurman once said, *"Don't ask what the world needs. Ask what makes you come alive and go do it. Because what the world needs is people who have come alive."*

This powerful truth echoes the importance of living with purpose. Like Viktor Frankl, Thurman understood that it's our inner drive—our reason for being—that fuels resilience in the face of adversity. Whether enduring unimaginable suffering or navigating everyday setbacks, those who are connected to their 'why' are more likely to persevere. We may never face the horrors of a concentration camp, but we all encounter moments of hardship—career disappointments, personal losses, or emotional battles. In those moments, our purpose is what breathes life into our efforts and guides us forward.

My Story

Like Frankl, I too had to learn that while I couldn't always control my circumstances, I could control my response. Years ago, I experienced moments when life's struggles felt overwhelming. My "why" was not always clear, and like many people, I often wondered why certain challenges came my way. The weight of uncertainty and setbacks threatened to shake my confidence, leaving me searching for something to hold onto. However, I soon learned that having a clear purpose could help me endure even the darkest moments. In those times of doubt, I reminded myself that every challenge could shape me rather than break me.

I created my personal mission statement, "I am" affirmations, and priority statements to help me stay focused on the bigger picture. Repeating these affirmations became more than just a habit—it became a declaration of the person I was becoming. When fear whispered that I wasn't enough, my affirmations spoke louder, reminding me of the strength within me. I adopted this practice after reading Joel Osteen's *The Power of I Am* and Stephen Covey's *The 7 Habits of Highly Effective People*. Their words reinforced my budding realization: the mind is a battlefield, and winning starts with the thoughts we choose to believe.

Here are a few examples of affirmations I repeat to myself every day:

"I am bold."
"I am brilliant."
"I am excellent."

There were days when these statements felt far from reality, when self-doubt tried to convince me otherwise. But I repeated them anyway, because I knew my words had power. While I'm lying down to sleep, driving, or starting my day, I repeat these statements to realign my mind and spirit with my purpose. I've learned that purpose isn't just about grand achievements—it's about the small, daily decisions to keep moving forward.

This practice has kept me grounded, especially during difficult times when the ups and downs of life threatened to knock me off course. It has reminded me that even when I feel lost, I could still choose to rise.

Looking back, I realize that this journey reshaped not just my mindset, but my entire approach to life. Adversity became my teacher, rather than my enemy, guiding me toward strength, resilience, and growth. Every challenge I faced refined my character, and each struggle became another stepping stone toward the person I was meant to become.

My experience taught me that, while I couldn't always control my circumstances, I could control my response. This realization reinforced my belief that our reaction to hardship shapes the trajectory of our lives, turning challenges into either roadblocks or stepping stones to growth and triumph.

Like Frankl and Schwarzenegger, I learned setbacks do not have to define us—they can be the very things that propel us forward. My affirmations and mission statement became more than just words; they became the foundation upon which I rebuilt my confidence, courage, and sense of purpose.

Adapt and Advance: The Power of Perspective

Life can feel chaotic when you lose sight of your "why." Challenges may seem insurmountable, and setbacks can shake your confidence. In these moments, it's easy to feel lost or overwhelmed. However, by keeping the big picture in front of you, you can regain control over your perspective and navigate difficulties with greater resilience.

Arnold Schwarzenegger once said, "The meaning of life is not simply to exist, to survive, but to move ahead, to go up, to achieve, to conquer."

Like Schwarzenegger and Viktor Frankl, I learned that setbacks are not roadblocks but stepping stones toward growth. Every difficulty carries the potential to shape and strengthen us, but only if we choose to see it that way. My affirmations and mission statement became the tools I used to adapt, advance, and keep moving forward, reinforcing the belief that purpose and perspective can transform any challenge.

While we cannot control what happens to us, we can control how we respond; and this determines whether we rise above our situation or remain stuck in its grip. Choosing to face challenges with a mindset of growth and resilience enables us to turn obstacles into opportunities.The key to maintaining this perspective is to keep your "why" at the center of your life. Without a clear purpose, you can easily lose focus or motivation when life becomes difficult. Your "why" serves as a guiding force, reminding you of what truly matters and giving you the strength to push forward even in the toughest moments.

Seven Steps to Discover Your "Why"

In *Start With Why: How Great Leaders Inspire Everyone to Take Action*, Simon Sinek underscores the transformative power of discovering your "why"—the core purpose, cause, or belief that fuels your actions. Your "why" is the foundation for personal fulfillment and effective leadership. Here are seven steps to help you uncover it:

1. Reflect on Your Past Experiences

Examine your life for recurring patterns in behaviors, decisions, and achievements that brought you joy and fulfillment. These moments often highlight the core values and beliefs shaping your purpose. By understanding what consistently inspires and motivates you, you can begin to uncover your "why."

For me, practicing medicine to improve patients' lives brings immense joy and fulfillment. I encourage you to identify what sparks that same sense of purpose in your own life.

2. Identify What You Stand For

Your "why" is deeply rooted in the values, causes, or principles you hold dear. Reflect on what truly matters to you and resonates at your core. Defining these values allows you to articulate a purpose that aligns with your beliefs and inspires others.

Having faced significant adversity, I am passionate about helping others overcome challenges by sharing principles that have proven effective in my own journey. When I do this, I experience a profound sense of joy and fulfillment.

3. Focus on Contribution, Not Success

Your "why" is not about personal achievements but about the value you bring to others. True purpose arises from contributing to something greater than yourself. Ask yourself how your work or actions can create a positive impact on others.

This philosophy shapes my mission statement, which emphasizes adding value and serving a greater cause. To uncover your "why," focus on a larger vision that resonates with and fulfills you.

4. Understand the Golden Circle

Sinek introduces the concept of the "Golden Circle," comprising three layers: Why, How, and What. While most people start with "what" (their actions) and work outward, successful leaders and organizations begin with "why" (their purpose). To discover your "why," start by asking why you do what you do, then align your "how" (methods) and "what" (actions) to support that purpose.

5. Seek Feedback from Others

Those who know you well—colleagues, friends, or family—can offer valuable perspectives on your strengths, passions, and patterns. Ask them what they think you excel at and what they believe inspires you. Their insights may help you identify aspects of your "why" that you might overlook.

6. Experiment and Iterate

Finding your "why" is a journey, often one involving trial and error. Experiment with various approaches and reflect on what feels authentic and fulfilling. As you gain clarity, refine your understanding of your purpose.

7. Articulate Your Why Clearly

Once you've discovered your "why," distill it into a clear, concise, and inspiring statement. This declaration serves as a guiding principle for your decisions, actions, and communication.

A well-defined "why" lays the groundwork for meaningful work, authentic relationships, and impactful leadership.

Discovering your "why" is not just an abstract exercise—it is a deeply personal journey shaped by experiences, values, and contributions. As I reflect on my own path, I see how these principles have influenced my life, guiding me toward a career of service and impact. My journey demonstrates how embracing purpose transforms challenges into opportunities for growth and fulfillment.

Since childhood, I have found immense joy in helping others, a passion that has shaped my career as a medical doctor and scientist. Reflecting on my past experiences, I see a consistent pattern—whether through practicing medicine, contributing to scientific research, or serving in my church, I have always been driven by a desire to make a meaningful impact.

This ties into Sinek's principle of *focusing on contribution, not success*. My "why" has never been about personal accolades but about the lives I can touch. Every diagnosis made, every research project pursued, and every act of service in my church reinforces my purpose—to add value to others and make a difference in their lives.

Additionally, my journey aligns with the principle of *identifying what you stand for*. Having faced personal adversity, I understand the transformative power of resilience, faith, and knowledge. This has fueled my commitment to not only help patients heal physically but also to empower them mentally and emotionally. I also embrace the concept of *experimenting and iterating* as my "why" continues to evolve. Every challenge I overcome and every new experience refines my understanding of my purpose, allowing me to adapt and grow. By consistently aligning my actions with my core beliefs, I find fulfillment, resilience, and the motivation to keep serving.

By following these steps, you can discover a purpose that not only drives you, but also inspires those around you.

Bible Verse and Explanation

"For I know the plans and thoughts that I have for you,' says the Lord, 'plans for peace and well-being and not for disaster, to give you a future and a hope." – Jeremiah 29:11 (AMP)

This verse is a reminder that God's plan for your life is filled with purpose. Even when your circumstances seem uncertain, trust that there is a greater picture. Your "why" is part of His divine plan, and every setback can be a setup for something greater.

Very Important Next Step

Write your personal mission statement, and list five "I am" affirmations that align with the person you aspire to become. Reflect on what drives you in both the short and long term, then write it down and keep it visible. Understanding your "why" provides clarity, focus, and motivation, helping you stay true to your core beliefs and make intentional decisions.

Taking time to identify your purpose will help you to stay resilient in the face of adversity, and ensure your actions align with your values. Find a quiet space to reflect, write about your purpose, and use affirmations if needed. Keep these reflections visible and revisit them daily to stay inspired, motivated, and aligned with your goals.

Worksheet or Exercise for Growth

Exercise 1: Define Your "Why"

- What is your long-term purpose?
- What is your short-term purpose for this season of life?
- Write five affirmations that align with your purpose (e.g., "I am strong," "I am focused").

Exercise 2: Mission Statement

- Create a personal mission statement that describes your purpose and values in one or two sentences.

Example: "My mission is to inspire and help others overcome challenges while growing in faith and resilience."

Keep your "why" visible in places where you'll see it daily—on your desk, in your journal, or on your phone. Repeat your affirmations often. Purpose is not something you find once; it's something you reaffirm every day.

Discovering your "why" equips you to endure life's challenges and overcome adversity. Victor Frankl's story, my personal journey, and the lessons of faith remind us that purpose fuels perseverance.

When life gets tough, hold on to your "why" and trust in God's plan. It's the anchor that will keep you steady, and the compass that guides you forward.

In the next chapter, we'll explore how to embrace failure as a stepping stone toward success and make your mess your message. Remember, every challenge has a purpose, and every setback can be a setup for your breakthrough.

CHAPTER 3

Your Mess, Your Message: Advancing and Adapting Against All Odds.

O bstacles are inevitable, but they don't define your journey—how you respond to them does. The truth is, every struggle, setback, and failure you face holds the potential to shape your message and inspire others. In this chapter, we will explore how to turn life's messes into messages of resilience, faith, and purpose; because when you choose to adapt and advance, your greatest trials can become your most powerful testimonies.

 By shifting your mindset, you can transform adversity into an opportunity for growth, resilience, and purpose. This chapter will empower you to see obstacles not as roadblocks, but as opportunities to grow, thrive, and comfort others, because with the right perspective, challenges can become stepping stones towards your purpose and personal breakthrough.

> "Obstacles don't have to stop you. If you run into a
> wall, don't turn around and give up. Figure out how
> to climb it, go through it, or work around it."
>
> – Michael Jordan.

Michael Jordan's words remind us that obstacles are not the end of the road but opportunities to find new paths forward. Many successful individuals have embodied this mindset, turning their greatest struggles into powerful messages of resilience and inspiration.

How this worked for successful people: Robin Roberts

Robin Roberts, a celebrated journalist, famously said, "Make your mess your message." Robin turned her battle with cancer into a platform of hope and inspiration for millions. Instead of hiding her struggle, she used it to encourage others facing similar challenges.

Her story is a testament to resilience—when we face adversity with courage and grace, we can turn even the most painful moments into opportunities to uplift others. Just like Robin, we all face struggles that seem overwhelming. But if we choose to share rather than hide them, our struggles can become a beacon of hope for others.

My Story

Like Robin Roberts, I too had to face moments of pain and uncertainty that could have silenced me. Instead of allowing my struggles to define me, I chose to embrace them, turning each setback into an opportunity for growth and purpose. Just as Robin used her battle with cancer to inspire millions, I have learned to transform my hardships into a message of resilience. My journey has been filled with challenges that tested my strength, but through faith and perseverance, I found a way to rise above them.

My journey is filled with "messes" that could have shattered me. At just seven years old, I lost my mother—a loss too profound for my young heart to understand. By 13, I was dealt another devastating blow when my father passed away, leaving me to navigate a world that suddenly felt colder, emptier. The weight of grief was suffocating, and the loneliness was unbearable. Yet, life did not pause for my pain—it kept moving, forcing me to move with it.

At 16, I failed high school chemistry. It wasn't just a bad grade; it felt like confirmation of my deepest fears—that I wasn't good enough, that maybe I wasn't cut out for success. At 17, I struggled through my pre-med exams, questioning whether the dream of becoming a doctor was slipping through my fingers. Medical school only added to the turmoil—at 21, failing pharmacology and pathology felt like yet another reminder of my inadequacies. Each failure chipped away at my confidence, and doubt began whispering in my ear, urging me to quit.

But the challenges didn't stop. At 36, I faced the daunting reality of transitioning to the United States, stepping into an unfamiliar world with new obstacles waiting at every turn. At 40, I failed the USMLE Step One exam—a crushing setback that made me wonder if I would ever achieve my dream. Then, at 43, another blow—I scored in the 10th percentile on my Psychiatry Resident In-Training Exam. Each of these moments felt like a good excuse to give up. The weight of repeated disappointments pressed down on me, tempting me to give in.

But I refused. Instead of letting my failures define me, I chose to rise. I learned to adapt and advance, even when the road ahead seemed impossible. Through every painful moment, I leaned on the comfort of God's promises, reminding myself that my story wasn't over, that I had a purpose greater than my setbacks. Through His grace, I have not only survived but thrived.

Now, I use my story to comfort and inspire others, to remind them that no failure is final and no challenge is insurmountable. If I can overcome it, so can you. No matter how many times life knocks you down, no matter how many times you feel like quitting—keep pushing forward. Your story isn't finished yet.

Adapt and Advance: See Challenges as Opportunities

2 Corinthians 1:3-4 (AMP) says: "Blessed [gratefully praised and adored] be the God and Father of our Lord Jesus Christ, the Father of mercies and the God of all comfort, who comforts us in all our troubles so that we may be able to comfort those who are in any kind of trouble with the comfort with which we ourselves are comforted by God."

This verse reminds us that God doesn't waste our pain. The comfort He gives us is meant to flow through us to help others. Your struggles are not in vain—they are opportunities to become a source of strength and hope for someone else. When you face challenges, view them as opportunities to grow, adapt, and find meaning. God's bigger plan is to transform your mess into a message of comfort and victory.

Life has a way of presenting challenges that feel insurmountable, but what if those challenges were actually opportunities in disguise? Imagine losing a job unexpectedly—what seems like the end of stability could be the gateway to discovering a passion, launching a new career, or pursuing something far more fulfilling.

When I scored in the 10th percentile on my Psychiatry Resident In-Training Exam (PRITE) during my first year of residency at 43, it felt like a crushing blow. Doubt crept in, and I questioned whether I was truly cut out for this path. But instead of letting failure define me, I chose to use the setback as fuel for growth. I sought out the secrets to mastering the exam, applied them rigorously, and worked harder than ever. The result? By my second year of residency, my score skyrocketed to the 84th percentile.

Recognizing that the strategies I used to climb from the 10th to the 84th percentile were effective, I knew they had the potential to help others as well. Determined to turn my struggle into a lesson of empowerment, I volunteered to lead PRITE preparation sessions for two classes below me in my third year. Not only did this allow me to lift others up, but it also refined my own knowledge, propelling my score to the 92nd percentile. Seeing the impact of these efforts, I knew there was more work to be done.

In my fourth year, I expanded my teachings to all classes in the program. By then, my percentile had risen to the 95th percentile, and at least four of the 32 residents in my program achieved scores at or above the 95th percentile nationally. What began as a personal setback became a transformative experience—one that reshaped my mindset, strengthened my resilience, and, most importantly, allowed me to uplift others on their journey. This experience reinforced a powerful truth: challenges are not meant to stop us; they are designed to refine us, push us forward, and give us the wisdom to help others do the same.

Dr. Martin Luther King Jr. once said, *"Our very survival depends on our ability to stay awake, to adjust to new ideas, to remain vigilant and to face the challenge of change."*

Growth demands that we embrace change rather than resist it. Henry Ford echoed a similar truth, stating, *"Obstacles are those frightful things you see when you take your eyes off your goal."* Our focus should never be on the obstacle itself, but on the path beyond it. The moment we shift our attention from the problem to the solution, we unlock our potential to overcome anything in our way.

This is the essence of faith and purpose. *2 Corinthians 1:3-4 (AMP)* highlights a profound truth: *"God uses our struggles to equip us to comfort others."* Our trials are not meaningless; they are stepping stones to a greater purpose. The pain we endure equips us to be a source of hope and encouragement to others walking similar paths. When we adapt and advance through adversity, we become living testimonies of God's grace. Every mess we endure has the potential to become a message that uplifts, empowers, and transforms lives. Take heart—your struggles are not in vain. They are preparing you to be a beacon of light for someone else.

7 Steps to Transforming Your Mess into Your Message

In The Gifts of Imperfection by Brené Brown, the concept of "make your mess your message" is woven into her guide for living a wholehearted life. Below are seven key steps drawn from her work, along with practical examples illustrating each point.

1. Embrace Vulnerability

To turn struggles into strength, you must first accept your imperfections and be willing to share them. Vulnerability is the birthplace of authenticity and connection. Brené Brown highlights how opening up about her own struggles with shame allowed her to deeply connect with others, making her work more relatable and transformative. Similarly, I openly share my experiences of failing exams to remind others that I am far from perfect. However, instead of letting these setbacks define me, I have chosen to persevere and move forward, using my experiences to encourage others on similar journeys.

2. Own Your Story

Acknowledging and taking responsibility for your experiences, no matter how messy, is vital. By owning your story, you reclaim your power and choose how it shapes you. Brené recounts confronting her perfectionism and learning to accept herself as she is, rather than who she thought she should be. I've made poor financial investments in the past, and while those mistakes were costly, I take full responsibility for them. Through diligence and discipline, I have worked to recover from my debts, and while I am not yet where I want to be financially, I am on the right path and committed to staying the course.

One example that illustrates this principle is my transition to the United States for my PhD, followed by a Postdoctoral Fellowship and then Residency—each step bringing immense growth but also significant financial burdens. The accumulated debts were substantial, but rather than feeling overwhelmed, I chose to take control of my financial future.

As soon as I had the opportunity to invest in retirement during residency, I opted for a higher contribution, knowing it would set the foundation for long-term financial stability. When moonlighting became an option, I seized it without hesitation. This decision has allowed me to invest more, gradually pay off some debts, and still provide for my family's immediate needs.

There is still a long way to go, but I am confident that I am on the right path. Every step I take is intentional, reinforcing my belief that while we may not always control our circumstances, our choices determine our progress and ultimate success.

3. Cultivate Self-Compassion

Transforming your mess into a message begins with kindness toward yourself. Self-compassion helps you process pain and build resilience. A reader of The Gifts of Imperfection by Brené Brown once shared how practicing self-compassion after a difficult divorce helped her move past self-blame and use her experience to mentor others. I have learned to extend this grace to myself as well. When my Canadian visa application was denied in 2012, preventing me from attending a conference, I chose to stay calm. I reapplied and, just days before the event, my visa was granted. However, even before that, I had already reassured myself that no matter the outcome, I would be okay. This mindset shift helped me accept setbacks without being overwhelmed by them.

4. Reframe Shame into Courage

Shame thrives in silence, but sharing your experiences with courage diminishes its power. Talking openly about challenges helps us see them not as personal failures but as opportunities for transformation. Brené Brown turned her personal pain into a meaningful contribution by conducting research on shame and vulnerability. Inspired by this, I chose to speak openly about scoring in the 10th percentile on my Psychiatry Resident In-Training Exam in 2021. Instead of hiding my struggles, I used them as a catalyst for change, working diligently to improve and ultimately excel. This openness not only helped me grow, but reminded me that setbacks are part of every success story.

5. Connect with Others

Sharing your story builds trust and fosters empathy. Your vulnerability can serve as a bridge for others facing similar struggles. A man who overcame substance use addiction used his story to inspire others at recovery meetings, proving that connection can turn personal pain into a tool for collective healing. Similarly, I have found that when I share my experiences, I create opportunities for deeper relationships, mentorship, and encouragement for those who need it most.

6. Focus on Growth, Not Perfection

Making your message your message isn't about crafting a polished success story—it's about authenticity and embracing the often messy process of growth. A woman struggling with body image started sharing her unfiltered journey online, empowering others to embrace their bodies and imperfections. By being honest about my own challenges, whether in academics, finances, or personal development, I remind myself and others that growth is a process, and progress is more important than perfection.

7. Let Your Story Inspire Action

Transforming your experience into a catalyst for positive change allows your struggles to serve a greater purpose. Rather than simply reflecting on hardships, we can use them to advocate, educate, and uplift others. Brené Brown's research and public talks on shame and vulnerability have inspired millions to embrace wholehearted living and foster deeper connections. Similarly, I have found purpose in using my own journey to help others overcome their struggles. In *The Gifts of Imperfection*, Brené Brown teaches that making your mess your message involves vulnerability, self-compassion, and connection. By owning our stories and using them to inspire growth and action, we can turn personal hardships into powerful messages of hope and resilience. When we embrace imperfection, we create a more authentic and meaningful life—not just for ourselves, but for those around us.

Very Important Next Step :
Turning Your Struggles into a Message of Hope

Take a moment to reflect on a personal struggle or challenge you have faced. How can you turn that experience into a message that empowers others? Your hardships, failures, and obstacles are not just difficulties to endure—they hold the potential to inspire and uplift those walking a similar path. By sharing your story, you remind others that they are not alone in their struggles, and that resilience is possible. Transforming your pain into a message of hope can help you heal while also contributing to the growth and strength of those around you.

To begin this process, identify a past challenge that has shaped who you are today. Find a quiet moment to reflect on the lessons it taught you and how it influenced your personal growth. Then, write down one way this story could help someone facing a similar challenge. You may choose to journal your thoughts, share your experience with a friend or colleague, or even post about it in a blog or on social media. By articulating your journey, you'll not only strengthen your own perspective but also empower others to keep moving forward.

Here are three simple steps to guide you in making your mess your message:

1. Reflect on a significant challenge or setback you have overcome.

2. Write down how this experience can be used to encourage or help someone else.

3. Share a word of comfort or encouragement with someone currently facing a difficult situation.

Your story has the power to bring hope, strength, and inspiration to others—embrace it, share it, and let it be a light for those in need.

Worksheet or Exercise for Growth

Exercise 1: Identify Your Mess

- List one or two major challenges or setbacks you have faced.
- Write down the lessons you learned from those experiences.

Exercise 2: Make Your Mess Your Message

- How can you use your story to encourage someone going through a similar challenge?
- Write a short message of comfort or hope based on your experience.

Example: "I failed an important exam, but I tried again and succeeded. You can, too. Failure is not the end—it's a stepping stone to your next success."

Remember, your story matters. God uses broken pieces to create a beautiful masterpiece. Your pain has a purpose, and your mess can become someone else's miracle. Keep adapting, keep advancing, and never give up.

Remember also, that your mess does not define you—it prepares you. Every setback you face can become part of a greater message of resilience, comfort, and hope. Just as God has comforted me through the loss of my parents and many failures, He will comfort you and equip you to inspire others. In the next chapter, "Failing Forward: Paying Tuition to the School of Life," we will explore how to embrace failure as a learning opportunity and a stepping stone to success.

CHAPTER 4

Failing Forward: Paying Tuition to the School of Life

Why did the scarecrow win an award? Because he was outstanding in his field—despite all the times he fell flat on his face.

Like the scarecrow, we all have moments when we fall flat on our faces. But what sets successful people apart is their ability to get back up, learn, and keep moving forward. In this chapter, you will learn how to turn failure into a stepping stone for success. Failure, as painful as it may seem, is not the end of the road, but a crucial part of the journey. By embracing failure as a teacher, you can build resilience, grow from setbacks, and move closer to achieving your goals.

Some of history's greatest achievements have emerged from moments of seemingly insurmountable failure. Embracing setbacks as opportunities for growth allows us to see failure not as defeat, but as "an essential part of the journey to success", as Albert Einstein once said.

How This Worked for Successful People: Richard Branson

Many of the world's most successful individuals like Richard Branson and Bill Gates have faced significant failures, yet they used these setbacks as stepping stones to greatness. Richard Branson, founder of the Virgin Group, once said, "Do not be embarrassed by your failures, learn from them and start again."

Branson's career is filled with risks that didn't always pan out. One of those risks was his venture into Virgin Cola which was a flop. Yet, instead of being paralyzed by failure, he chose to view it as a learning experience, refining his approach to business and going on to build a billion-dollar empire.

 Bill Gates also faced failure before launching Microsoft, proving that setbacks are often prerequisites for success. Bill Gates also reminds us, "It's fine to celebrate success, but it is more important to heed the lessons of failure." One of Gates' early setbacks was a failed business venture called Traf-O-Data. He learned from his mistakes in that attempt, and used them as a foundation for future success. Just like Branson and Bill Gates, we all encounter failures. But what separates those who succeed from those who don't is the ability to extract lessons from failure and move forward with renewed determination.

7 Steps to Failing Forward: Turning Mistakes into Stepping Stones for Success.

1. Embrace Curiosity Over Conformity

Curiosity drives innovation and resilience, and allows individuals to see opportunities in failure rather than obstacles. Albert Einstein's refusal to conform to rote learning led to his expulsion from school. Instead of succumbing to this 'setback', he pursued self-directed study, eventually developing revolutionary theories that redefined physics.

Leaving Nigeria at the height of my career as an attending physician to start afresh in the United States showed my commitment to curiosity over conformity. I was driven by the belief that greater opportunities and experiences awaited beyond my comfort zone.

In my case, conformity would have meant staying with the status quo—remaining in Nigeria as a Consultant Physician, the equivalent of an Attending Physician in the U.S. On the surface, it seemed like the logical and comfortable choice. I had already reached a prestigious position, and many would have seen no reason to leave.

But I knew deep in my heart that God had more in store for me, a purpose that required additional training and experience in the United States. I refused to conform to what was expected or easy. I vividly remember one of my professors in Nigeria questioning my decision: *"Why would you leave a place where you can easily make money for a country where you have to work hard for every single dollar?"*

That statement didn't deter me—it reinforced my resolve. I was never afraid of hard work or stepping into the unknown. I knew that growth often comes through challenges, and I was willing to take that leap of faith. So, I moved, embracing the journey ahead with determination and trust in God's plan.

2. Persist Despite Early Failures

Persistence in the face of rejection and obstacles turns failure into progress. Richard Branson's early venture, a student magazine, was unprofitable. But he persevered, launching Virgin Records, which became a massive success and laid the foundation for the Virgin Group.

Although I am a physician today, my journey has been marked by numerous setbacks, beginning in elementary school when I failed to gain admission into prestigious Federal Government Colleges for Middle/High School in Nigeria. Despite these challenges, I have remained steadfast, turning each failure into a stepping stone toward success.

3. Question Assumptions

Challenging established norms and beliefs is essential for innovation and progress. Bill Gates dropped out of Harvard to pursue his vision of a personal computer in every home. By questioning the assumption that computers were only for large institutions, he co-founded Microsoft, transforming the tech industry.

One assumption I challenged was the belief that conducting substantial research as a psychiatry resident would be nearly impossible due to time constraints and the lack of a strong research infrastructure at my institution. By strategically managing my time, I successfully published over 12 manuscripts, presented at more than 12 scientific conferences, and secured funding for at least two grant applications during my four years of residency. This experience demonstrated that with determination and effective prioritization, significant academic and research achievements are possible, even in resource-limited environments.

4. Learn from Criticism

Constructive criticism offers insights that refine ideas and approaches, turning missteps into learning opportunities. Oprah Winfrey was fired from her first television job after being told she was "unfit for TV." Instead of giving up, she learned from the experience, honed her skills, and created one of the most successful talk shows in history. I accept feedback with grace and move on, recognizing that every critique carries the potential for growth and improvement.

5. Adapt and Reassess

Adapting plans based on feedback and new information ensures continuous progress even after setbacks. Thomas Edison famously failed thousands of times before perfecting the light bulb. Instead of seeing these as failures, he viewed them as necessary experiments, saying, "I have not failed. I've just found 10,000 ways that won't work." Like Edison, I have learned that persistence heavily requires adjusting and refining strategies based on lessons learned so as to make meaningful progress.

6. Collaborate and Seek Diverse Perspectives

Working with others and valuing diverse viewpoints fosters innovation and problem-solving. Steve Jobs, after being ousted from Apple, founded NeXT and collaborated with Pixar. These ventures taught him the value of teamwork, and when he returned to Apple, he leveraged these lessons to build iconic products like the iPhone. By surrounding myself with mentors, colleagues, and researchers from different backgrounds, I have discovered that collaboration enhances creativity and leads to stronger, more impactful solutions.

7. Focus on the Long-Term Impact

True success often lies in creating a lasting legacy rather than seeking immediate results. Marie Curie, despite financial and social challenges, persisted in her research on radioactivity.

Her dedication not only earned her two Nobel Prizes but also revolutionized medicine and science, impacting generations to come. Einstein's story and those of other great minds like Branson, Gates, and Curie demonstrate that failing forward requires curiosity, resilience, and adaptability. By reframing failures as opportunities for growth, anyone can transform setbacks into stepping stones toward enduring success.

Growing and becoming resilient isn't reserved for the world's greatest minds, rather it's a never ending process we have to undergo as long as we aim to be better. Failure, as painful and disheartening as it can be, has the power to break us or build us—depending on how we choose to respond. Just as Curie, Einstein, Branson, and Gates turned their setbacks into stepping stones, I, too, have faced moments when failure felt like an unbearable weight pressing down on me.

20007 was a year of high hopes and crushing disappointments—I remember it like it was yesterday. I had poured my hard-earned money into investments I believed in, only to watch them crumble before my eyes. The stock market collapsed, and with it, a significant portion of my financial security. As if that wasn't enough, a family business I had invested in also failed to deliver the returns I had envisioned. Like a double blow, it knocked the wind out of me.

The sting of those losses ran deep. I questioned my decisions, wrestled with self-doubt, and wondered if I would ever recover. But amid the frustration and regret, I made a choice—I refused to let those setbacks define me. Instead, I saw those setbacks as tuition paid to the school of life. The lessons were costly, but they were also invaluable. Slowly, I rebuilt. I learned. I adapted. And over time, I transformed my approach to financial decisions, realizing that every stumble, no matter how painful, was bringing me closer to true mastery.

Adapt and Advance

The failures I faced taught me a key principle: resilience. Falling is inevitable, but staying down is a choice. **Micah 7:8 (Amplified Bible)** beautifully captures this: *"Do not rejoice over me, O enemy; for though I fall, I will rise; though I sit in darkness, the Lord is a light for me."*

This verse became a guiding light in my darkest moments, reminding me that failure was not the end of my story—it was a chapter, not the conclusion. Every loss, every disappointment, and every painful setback forced me to reassess, recalibrate, and grow in ways I never imagined. I began to understand that setbacks were not roadblocks, but detours guiding me toward a better path. Failure is a teacher—it shows you what doesn't work so you can refine your approach. And just as Proverbs 24:16 (AMP) says, *"For a righteous man falls seven times and rises again, but the wicked stumble in time of disaster and collapse,"* I realized that my ability to rise each time I fell was what would define my journey, not the failures themselves.

By embracing this mindset, I learned how to adapt—to see opportunities where I once saw dead ends. Instead of allowing my financial losses to paralyze me, I studied market trends, sought mentorship, and refined my approach. Instead of viewing the failure of the family business as a personal defeat, I examined what went wrong, identified critical lessons, and used them to make smarter investment decisions in the future. Resilience is built through adversity—every time you rise after falling, you grow stronger. The wisdom of Proverbs 24:16 reassured me that falling wasn't failure; it was simply part of the journey. God does not promise that we will never face challenges, but He does promise that when we do, we will have the strength to rise again.

More than just financial wisdom, these experiences reshaped how I approached life's challenges. They strengthened my ability to persevere in my medical journey, research endeavors, and personal growth. I understood that success isn't about avoiding failure but about developing the grit to rise every time you fall.

Success is a process—as Einstein said, "Failure is success in progress." And through it all, I clung to the truth that, though I may stumble, I will not stay down. Micah 7:8 reminds us that even in our darkest moments, God is our light, guiding us forward. When you adapt to your circumstances and advance despite the setbacks, you don't just survive—you emerge stronger, wiser, and more prepared for whatever comes next.

Worksheet or Exercise for Growth.

Reflection Worksheet: Turning Failures into Lessons

1. List three failures or setbacks you've experienced.

2. For each, write down:

- What happened?
- The emotions you felt.
- One lesson you learned.

3. Create an action plan for how you'll approach similar situations differently in the future.

Failure is a universal experience, but it doesn't define you. By choosing to rise, learn, and grow, you turn every setback into a stepping stone. Keep moving forward!

Very Important Next Step

Reflecting daily on a mistake or setback, and writing down a lesson learned from it can be a powerful tool for growth. By taking the time to do this, you give yourself opportunities to turn failures into valuable learning experiences. Every mistake holds the potential to teach you something meaningful about yourself, your approach, and your goals. Embracing these lessons will make you more resilient and adaptable, thereby improving your ability to navigate future challenges better. Recognizing what went wrong allows you to refine your strategies, making you better prepared for what lies ahead. Journaling your reflections further reinforces this process, enabling you to track progress and develop a mindset that views failure as an essential part of your success journey.

Each evening, take five minutes to journal about a mistake or setback from your day or week. Start by describing what happened, including the circumstances and your emotional response. Then, shift your focus to what you learned from the experience. Ask yourself: *What could I have done differently? What did this setback teach me?* Finally, identify one concrete action you can take next time to avoid repeating the same mistake. This simple practice of reflection will help you see each failure not as a roadblock, but as a stepping stone toward success.

To make this habit even more effective, follow this three-step process: First, write down what went wrong. Next, note the lesson you learned. Finally, commit to one action you'll take differently next time. By making reflection a regular part of your routine, you'll start to view setbacks not as failures, but as opportunities for growth, bringing you closer to your goals with each step forward.

Failure is not the end; it's a stepping stone to success. Remember, the key is to rise every time you fall, armed with the lessons learned. As you move forward, keep this truth in mind: It does not matter where you have come from; it only matters where you want to go.

CHAPTER 5

It Does Not Matter Where You Have Come From, It Only Matters Where You Want to Go.

D o you ever feel like your past is holding you back? The truth is, your future is shaped by what you do today, not by where you've been. Imagine standing at a crossroads, with one path leading toward the life you've always dreamed of and the other keeping you bound by the limitations of your past. The weight of where you've been may feel heavy, but the truth is, your past does not define you.

What matters is the direction you choose to take from this moment forward. Every great success story begins with someone who refused to let their circumstances dictate their destiny. No matter how difficult your journey has been, the power to shape your future is in your hands. In this chapter, you will discover the power of vision and belief in shaping your future, no matter your past. Your beginnings do not determine your destiny. What matters is your willingness to embrace growth, push past limitations, and focus on where you want to go. The road ahead is defined not by where you started, but by the choices you make moving forward. As Dean Graziosi wisely reminds us, your focus should be on the destination, not the starting point.

"It does not matter where you have come from.
It only matters where you want to go."

—Dean Graziosi

How This Worked for Successful People: Dean Graziosi

In **Dean Graziosi's** book *Millionaire Success Habits*, he shares the story of **John**, a man who was constantly told he would never amount to anything. The voices around him tried to limit his future before he even had a chance to shape it. Instead of accepting those words as truth, John made a different choice—he refused to let his past or other people's opinions dictate his destiny.

Rather than dwelling on where he started, **John focused on where he wanted to go**. He set his sights on a future greater than the limitations placed on him, worked relentlessly toward his goals, and eventually built an incredibly successful life. His story is proof that your circumstances do not define you—**your choices do**.

What decision can you make today to start shaping your own future? Just like John, you have the power to rise above any limiting narrative from your past. **Your past is just a chapter, not the whole book.** The key to unlocking your potential lies in directing your focus toward where you want to go and refusing to let anything hold you back.

How to focus on where you want to be

Your past doesn't define you; your actions today do. Below are the steps with real-life examples for each.

1. Define Your Vision with Clarity

Your future is shaped by the vision you hold for yourself. Without a clear destination, it's easy to drift through life, settling for whatever comes your way. Take time to write down exactly where you want to go—professionally, financially, and personally. Focus on the life you desire rather than where you currently are. A compelling vision serves as a compass, helping you recognize opportunities and take deliberate action toward your dreams.

Oprah Winfrey, born into poverty and faced with immense adversity, refused to let her circumstances dictate her future. She envisioned a career in media and worked relentlessly until she became a global media icon. **Arnold Schwarzenegger**, growing up in a small Austrian village, saw beyond his humble beginnings and set a bold vision for himself—to become a bodybuilding champion, a Hollywood star, and later, a U.S. governor. **Sara Blakely**, once a door-to-door fax machine salesperson, envisioned a future in entrepreneurship and built Spanx into a billion-dollar brand. Like them, you have the power to craft a vision so strong that it pulls you forward, no matter your starting point.

2. Focus on Daily Habits

A grand vision alone is not enough, as it's the small, daily habits that turn dreams into reality. Break down your big goals into manageable actions and commit to consistent progress. Dedicating even 30 minutes a day to learning, networking, or building a skill can compound into incredible growth over time. **J.K. Rowling**, while struggling as a single mother, didn't wait for the perfect moment to write—she squeezed in time whenever she could, one chapter at a time, until she built the billion-dollar *Harry Potter* empire. **Michael Jordan**, known for his relentless work ethic, practiced longer and harder than anyone else, turning himself into one of the greatest athletes of all time. **Elon Musk**, long before he became synonymous with Tesla and SpaceX, devoted himself to learning programming and engineering daily, laying the foundation for the revolutionary companies he would later create. The lesson? Success isn't about one big moment; it's about showing up every day and doing the work, especially when no one is watching.

3. Reframe Limiting Beliefs

The biggest obstacles to success often come from within. If you tell yourself, *I can't because of my past*, you've already lost before you even begin. Instead, shift your mindset to say, *My past has prepared me for growth.* By reframing limiting beliefs, you take control of your future and open yourself up to new possibilities.

Tony Robbins, who grew up in a broken and abusive home, refused to let his painful upbringing define him. Instead, he used his experiences as fuel to inspire millions, becoming one of the world's most influential motivational speakers. **Howard Schultz**, raised in a poor neighborhood, didn't let his circumstances limit him—he believed in his vision of creating a premium coffee culture, which ultimately led to the global success of Starbucks. **Nick Vujicic**, born without arms and legs, could have easily been consumed by despair, but he chose to see his physical limitations as a platform to inspire others, becoming a globally recognized speaker and author.

The way you frame your experiences can either hold you back or propel you forward. Choose to see setbacks as stepping stones rather than roadblocks.By defining a clear vision, committing to daily habits, and reframing limiting beliefs, you can succeed no matter where you come from. Whether you're inspired by Oprah's unwavering focus, Jordan's discipline, or Vujicic's resilience, remember this: your past does not dictate your future—it is simply a starting point on the journey to the life you truly desire.

My Story

Growing up, I faced numerous challenges and heard limiting narratives about what I could or could not achieve. Losing my parents at a young age added layers of difficulty to my journey. At times, the weight of grief and uncertainty felt suffocating, as if life had already decided my limits before I had a chance to define them myself. Yet, I held on to a vision of a better future, refusing to let my circumstances dictate my destiny. In those moments of doubt, I reminded myself that every great success story begins with resilience—the ability to rise despite the storm.

I vividly remember how pursuing higher education seemed like a distant dream, yet I never gave up on that dream. There were nights I stayed up studying with an empty stomach, moments when self-doubt crept in, whispering that I wasn't good enough. But I pushed forward, fueled by the belief that my future could be different. With determination, I earned a medical degree, a PhD, and even awards along the way. Every milestone became a testament to the power of perseverance—a reminder that struggle is not the enemy, but the catalyst for growth. My journey wasn't easy, but it was proof that your origins don't determine your potential.

This experience shaped my mindset, reinforcing the idea that success is built on vision, discipline, and resilience—the same principles embodied by figures like Oprah, Jordan, and Vujicic. Like them, I learned that challenges are not barriers but bridges to something greater. This philosophy aligns with the "Adapt and Advance" principle, teaching me that setbacks are not stop signs, but opportunities to recalibrate and keep moving forward.

Reflecting on my journey, I see how every challenge strengthened me, and deepened my determination. The loss, the struggle, and the uncertainty all became stepping stones, leading me to a future

I once thought was out of reach. To anyone feeling trapped by their circumstances, I offer this truth: your story is still being written, and you hold the pen.

Lessons from Vision and Belief

Your journey is not defined by where you started—it is shaped by where you choose to go. Too often, people allow their past failures, hardships, or circumstances to become the walls that confine them, limiting their potential before they've even begun. But the truth is, your past is not your final destination. It is merely the launching pad from which you rise. Many of the world's most successful individuals began with nothing—facing poverty, loss, rejection, or failure—but they refused to let those struggles write the final chapter of their lives.

The **Adapt and Advance** principle teaches us that setbacks are not permanent roadblocks; they are lessons disguised as detours, pushing us toward something greater. The key is to reframe past struggles as stepping stones, to recognize that each hardship holds wisdom, and to take deliberate action toward the life you desire. You are not bound by what has been; you are propelled by the vision of what could be.

Without vision, life can feel like wandering through a maze—endless twists and turns, uncertainty at every corner. But when you define your vision with clarity, you create a roadmap that helps you navigate life's challenges with purpose. A compelling vision is what keeps you moving forward when obstacles arise; it becomes the force that pulls you through adversity.

The Adapt and Advance philosophy emphasizes the importance of looking beyond past struggles and focusing on what lies ahead. Isaiah 43:18-19 reminds us, *"Do not remember the former things, or ponder the things of the past. Listen carefully, I am about to do a new thing.*"

This scripture reinforces the idea that the past is behind us, and a new path is always waiting to unfold. When you see your future vividly—whether it's a successful career, a thriving business, or a life filled with purpose—you begin to align your daily actions with that vision. Small, consistent steps lead to remarkable transformations. Just like a traveler with a map, a strong vision keeps you on course, reminding you why you started and giving you the strength to persevere.

Yet, even with a vision, fear can hold you captive—whispering doubts, magnifying risks, and keeping you from taking the next step. But faith is more powerful than fear. Faith gives you the courage to take action, even when you can't yet see the outcome. Every challenge presents two choices: to retreat in fear or to move forward in faith.

Philippians 3:13-14 urges us to *"forget what lies behind and reach forward to what lies ahead."* That forward motion is an act of faith, a declaration that you believe in your ability to grow and thrive despite challenges. The Adapt and Advance mindset teaches that success is not about waiting for perfect conditions; it's about pressing forward, knowing that growth happens in the journey, not just at the destination. Every setback contains a lesson, every obstacle builds resilience, and every moment of doubt is an opportunity to trust yourself and push forward.

No matter where you have been, your story is still being written. Your past does not have the power to define you—only your actions today do. By embracing the principles of vision, belief, and faith over fear, you take control of your future. Let go of what no longer serves you, focus on the path ahead, and trust that every step forward brings you closer to the life you were meant to live.

Worksheet or Exercise for Growth

Reflection Worksheet: Mapping Your Vision

1. Write down where you are today in key areas of life (career, relationships, health, spirituality).

2. Describe where you want to be in each area.

3. List three steps you can take this week to move toward your vision.

4. Reflect on one Bible verse or motivational quote that inspires you to keep going.

The power to change your future lies in your hands. Focus on what you can control, believe in the possibilities ahead, and trust that God will guide your steps. Keep moving forward!

Very Important Next Step

Every great transformation begins with a single, intentional step. Spend just five minutes each day visualizing the future you want and writing down one action you can take to move closer to it. This simple yet powerful practice aligns your daily actions with your vision, helping you bridge the gap between where you are and where you want to be.

By committing to this daily habit, you shift your focus from past setbacks to future possibilities. Visualization is not just wishful thinking—it's a tool used by some of the most successful people to bring their dreams to life. As Dean Graziosi and others have shown, your past does not dictate your destiny; your ability to see beyond it and take consistent action does. Every small step you take contributes to building a better future, reinforcing your resilience, and keeping you motivated even through life's challenges.

Find a quiet space each morning or evening, close your eyes, and vividly imagine where you want to be in one year, five years, or even ten years. Picture yourself achieving your goals, thriving, and living the life you envision. Then, turn that vision into reality by identifying one specific action you can take today to move closer to it. It doesn't have to be a massive leap—maybe it's sending an email, making a phone call, or dedicating time to learning a new skill. Over time, these small actions will create momentum, turning progress into an unstoppable force.

Most importantly, focus on progress, not perfection. Each day, commit to taking one positive step forward, no matter how small. Success isn't about giant leaps—it's about showing up for yourself every single day. Your future is shaped by what you do today, and every step you take is a declaration that your dreams are worth pursuing.

Your past may have taught you lessons, but it is your vision for the future that will drive your success. No matter where you're starting from, remember: it does not matter where you have come from; it only matters where you want to go. As you continue your journey, we'll explore how to face life's deep waters without getting drowned.

CHAPTER 6

Going Through the Deep Waters Without Getting Drowned

Why did the sailor bring a map into the stormy ocean? Because even in rough waters, it's important to know where you're going. Just like a sailor relies on a map to navigate turbulent waters, we need guiding principles to withstand life's storms. When challenges rise like towering waves, having the right mindset and tools can mean the difference between sinking in despair and pushing forward with resilience.

There are moments in life when the weight of adversity feels unbearable—like being pulled under by relentless waves, struggling to catch your breath. The overwhelming pain, uncertainty, and setbacks can make you feel as though you're drowning with no lifeline in sight. But what if the deep waters you fear are not meant to destroy you? What if they are the very forces that will shape you into someone stronger, wiser, and more resilient? The difference between sinking and surviving is not the absence of storms, but the ability to navigate them with faith, resilience, and the determination to keep moving forward.

In this chapter, you will learn how to navigate life's most challenging seasons—those "deep waters" that threaten to overwhelm us.

You'll discover the principles of resilience, the power of faith, and actionable steps to overcome life's adversities.

The greatest growth often comes from the most difficult struggles, shaping us in ways calm waters never could. As Franklin D. Roosevelt wisely reminds us, adversity is not an enemy but a teacher, forging strength and resilience in those who dare to face the storm.

> "Smooth seas never made a skilled sailor."
>
> – Franklin D. Roosevelt

Adversity has a way of testing our strength, revealing what we are truly capable of when faced with life's storms. History is filled with individuals who turned their struggles into stepping stones, proving that resilience is often forged in the face of hardship—just as Oprah Winfrey did.

How This Worked for Successful People: Oprah Winfrey

Oprah Winfrey's journey is one of resilience, determination, and an unshakable belief in her own potential. Born into poverty in rural Mississippi, she faced years of hardship, including a traumatic childhood marked by abuse and instability. At times, her circumstances seemed impossible to overcome—bouncing between caregivers, enduring deep emotional wounds, and struggling to find her place in the world. But Oprah refused to let her pain define her. Instead, she held on to the vision of a brighter future, and was determined to rise above her past.

One of her greatest tests came early in her career when she was told she was *"unfit for television."* The words stung, yet she refused to accept them as truth. Instead of allowing rejection to break her, she used it as fuel to refine her craft. She sharpened her skills, developed her unique voice, and embraced the power of authentic storytelling. Slowly, the world began to take notice.

Through relentless perseverance, Oprah not only proved her critics wrong, but went on to become one of the most influential media moguls of all time. Her story is a testament to the power of resilience, showing that even the deepest pain can be transformed into purpose, and rejection can be the catalyst for greatness

My Story.

Like Oprah Winfrey, I too had my share of profound hardships at an early age—challenges that could have easily defined my future. But rather than allowing pain and loss to consume me, I chose to hold on to faith, believing that my story was still being written.

Losing my mother at just seven years old and my father at thirteen shattered my world in ways words can hardly capture. The pain was raw, the emptiness unbearable. Their absence left behind not just emotional wounds, but a cascade of financial, educational, and psychological struggles that felt impossible to overcome. There were days when grief burned like fire in my chest and nights when loneliness felt like being swallowed by a bottomless sea. I often wondered how I would make it through, how I would find my way without them, how life could ever make sense again.

It has now been thirty-nine years since I lost Mommy, as I lovingly called her. She passed away on February 13, 1986, at just thirty-two years old, under painful and mysterious circumstances. I was only a child, too young to comprehend the weight of her passing, but I knew enough to feel the gaping void she left behind. My last memory of her is one I cherish deeply—her radiant smile, her face full of warmth and purpose, dressed in her pristine white nurse's uniform as she left for work at General Hospital Kontagora, Niger State, Nigeria, on that fateful morning. She was heavily pregnant, and though I have long assumed that both she and my unborn sister died due to pregnancy complications, possibly antepartum hemorrhage, the exact cause no longer matters. What matters is how profoundly her absence shaped our lives.

Her death was an earthquake that shattered our family. My father, a pharmacist, was utterly broken by losing her. He tried to carry on, but the weight of his grief was unbearable. Life dealt us yet another devastating blow when Daddy passed away on December 2, 1991. I still remember the words that escaped my lips when I learned of his death:

"Why would both of you bring us into this world only to leave us behind so soon?"

It was the desperate cry of a grieving child, lost in a sea of sorrow, pleading for answers that never came. To this day, those answers remain unknown. Yet, I have learned to live my best life without needing to understand everything. Some questions, I have come to accept, will remain unanswered.

Life without Mommy and Daddy was unimaginably hard. The pain, the loneliness, the struggle—it all felt insurmountable at times. There were moments when it seemed like the world had turned its back on me, like I was walking through fire with no way out or drowning in waters too deep to navigate. But in my darkest moments, when despair threatened to consume me, I clung to something greater than my pain—I clung to God's promises. Isaiah 43:2 (AMP) became my anchor:

"When you pass through the waters, I will be with you;
And through the rivers, they will not overwhelm you.
When you walk through fire, you will not be scorched,
Nor will the flame burn you."

I realized that no matter how fierce the storm, I was never alone. God's presence was my lifeboat, carrying me when I had no strength left to swim. The deep waters of loss did not drown me, and the fires of hardship did not consume me. Instead, they refined me, shaping me into someone stronger—someone who could rise again.

Today, I wear a wristband engraved with three words, each a testament to their lasting legacy. The first is ABASO, a tribute to my father, Adetunji Babatunde Solomon, and the name of his two businesses, ABASO Pharmacy and ABASO Hospital, both in Kontagora, Niger State, Nigeria. Both businesses ceased to exist shortly after his passing, but their memory lives on. The second is ESOB, my mother's name—Esther Omonike Babatunde—which also adorned the Block Making Industry my father started in her honor, another venture that did not survive long after his death. The third is ILF3—"I live for three." This phrase is my compass, my guiding principle. It reminds me that my journey is not mine alone. I live for Mommy, for Daddy, and for myself. I carry the dreams they could not fulfill, and every day, I strive to honor the foundation they laid for me.

The greatest gift Mommy and Daddy ever gave me was faith—faith in God through Jesus Christ. That faith, planted deep within me, has been my anchor. It has never failed me, not even in the darkest of times. It is the light that continues to guide me, just as their love and legacy continue to inspire me.

I believe that Daddy and Mommy look down on us with pride, knowing that their sacrifices were not in vain. We are here. We are thriving. We carry their love in our hearts and their legacy in our lives. I take comfort in knowing that they now rest peacefully in the bosom of our Lord Jesus Christ, and one day, we will meet again—never to part.

I have shared these details with one purpose in mind: to encourage anyone navigating the deep waters of grief and loss. When you lose a loved one, life can feel unbearably hard. The weight of sorrow may seem too heavy to bear, and you may wonder if you'll ever feel whole again. But I want you to know this: it is possible to move forward. Moving forward does not mean forgetting. It means finding the strength to carry their love and memory with you as you take each step.

Let my story remind you that the human spirit is resilient. You can heal. You can adapt. And you can thrive, even in the wake of unimaginable pain. No matter how deep the loss, there is still so much life to live, and so much purpose to fulfill.

Keep going—you are not alone.

Adapt and Advance: The Keys to Navigating Life's Deep Waters

No matter how dark or overwhelming life becomes, remember that God walks with you through every challenge, every loss, and every moment of uncertainty. When the weight of grief or hardship feels unbearable, it can be easy to believe that you have been abandoned, that no one sees your pain, or that you must carry your burdens alone. But that is far from the truth. God's presence is unwavering, even in your most difficult moments. Isaiah 43:2 serves as a powerful reminder of this truth:

"When you pass through the waters, I will be with you;
And through the rivers, they will not overwhelm you.
When you walk through fire, you will not be scorched,
Nor will the flame burn you."

The deep waters in this passage symbolize the overwhelming challenges we face—grief, loss, uncertainty, failure—while the fire represents the trials that test and refine us. God's promise is not that we will never face hardships, but that they will not consume us because His presence is our refuge and strength. Even when the storm is raging, even when you can't see a way forward, He is there, walking beside you. His presence gives you the strength to keep moving forward, even when everything in you wants to give up.

When life feels like too much to handle, take one step at a time. It's natural to feel overwhelmed when you look at the enormity of a problem or the uncertainty of the future. But instead of trying to solve everything at once, focus on what you can control today. The journey through hardship is not about taking massive leaps; it's about small, consistent steps forward.

If today all you can do is get out of bed, pray, or take one small action toward healing, that is enough. The path ahead may not always be clear, but faith is about trusting that each step will lead you exactly where you need to be.

In moments of struggle, lean on a support system. You were never meant to walk this journey alone. God places people in our lives to uplift, encourage, and strengthen us—whether it's family, friends, a faith community, or even a mentor. The burden becomes lighter when shared. There is strength in vulnerability, in admitting that you need help, and in allowing others to walk beside you in your pain. Surround yourself with those who remind you of God's faithfulness, who lift you up in prayer, and who stand with you when you feel like you can't stand on your own.

No struggle lasts forever, and no storm will rage indefinitely. Though the deep waters may feel endless, they will not drown you. Though the fire may feel unbearable, it will not consume you. You are not alone, and you never have to be. God's presence is your anchor, your strength, and your assurance that no matter what you face, you will rise again.

Worksheet or Exercise for Growth

1. List Your Deep Waters: Write down three challenges you've faced or are currently facing.

2. Reflect on God's Promises: Next to each challenge, write a Bible verse or personal affirmation that encourages you.

3. Action Plan: For each challenge, list one daily step you can take to navigate it.

Remember, resilience is built through action, faith, and reflection.

Life's deep waters are not meant to drown you but to strengthen you. Keep paddling!

Very Important Next Step

Life's deepest waters can feel overwhelming, but even in the midst of challenges, there are always signs of hope. Each morning, take 5–10 minutes to reflect on one challenge you have faced and one sign of progress in your life. Write them down in a journal or say them aloud as a personal affirmation. This simple but powerful practice shifts your focus from fear to faith, reminding you that difficulties do not define you—your response does.

Acknowledging past victories fosters resilience. Just as Oprah Winfrey overcame adversity by keeping her eyes on the future, you too can strengthen your mindset by focusing on the progress you've made. Isaiah 43:2 reassures us that even when we walk through deep waters, we will not be overwhelmed because God's presence is with us. This daily reflection builds gratitude, renews faith, and reinforces that even the smallest steps forward are proof that you are growing, however slow the process may seem.

To implement this, find a quiet space in the morning. Take a deep breath and recall a challenge you have already overcome—this serves as a reminder of your strength. Next, identify one thing, no matter how small, that gives you hope today. Write them in a journal or voice-record them on your phone. If you are religious, pair this reflection with a Bible verse like Isaiah 43:2. Over time, this practice will train your mind to see resilience and faith as natural responses to adversity.

Each day, commit to moving forward—even in the smallest way. Write down one actionable step you can take to navigate a current challenge, and recognize one way you see God's hand guiding you through. Life's struggles may feel vast, but with faith, resilience, and intentional steps forward, you will not only survive the deep waters—you will rise above them.

Life's challenges may feel like deep waters, but with faith, resilience, and actionable steps, you can navigate them without drowning. As we journey through difficulties, writing and journaling become essential tools to process, reflect, and thrive. In the next chapter, we'll explore how journaling can help you adapt and advance, even against all odds.

CHAPTER 7

Act of Journaling Through Difficulties to Adapt and Advance Against All Odds

I t's all too common for us to feel lost, overwhelmed, and uncertain about our future in those moments when life hits us particularly hard. But what if there was a simple yet powerful tool to help us find clarity, strength, and direction in those moments? What if we decide to journal? Journaling is more than just writing—it's a way to process pain, reflect on growth, and transform setbacks into stepping stones.

Through the act of putting pen to paper, we gain insight into our emotions, fears, and the paths before us. By recording our thoughts and experiences, we create a roadmap that guides us toward healing, resilience, and personal growth.

In this chapter, you will learn the transformative power of journaling as a tool for navigating life's toughest challenges. You'll discover how writing your thoughts, prayers, and reflections can help you adapt, advance, and thrive—even in the face of adversity. Through journaling, your thoughts take shape, giving you a clearer perspective on your journey and the strength to move forward.

"Writing is the painting of the voice."

– Voltaire

Writing is more than words—it is a form of expression that brings clarity, depth, and meaning to our experiences.Writing is more than ink on paper—it is a way to give voice to our deepest thoughts and experiences. Throughout history, some of the greatest minds have turned to journaling as a means of gaining clarity, resilience, and direction in the face of life's challenges.

How This Worked for Successful People: Marcus Aurelius, Seneca, and Epictetus

Throughout history, great thinkers like Marcus Aurelius, Seneca, and Epictetus have used journaling to reflect, plan, and navigate their lives. In his book Resilience, the swimmer talks about journaling as a common practice among these philosophers. Journaling allowed them to process emotions, clarify their thoughts, and build resilience against life's challenges.

My Story

Like Marcus Aurelius, I too took to writing as a means of processing deep emotions and finding clarity in difficult times. Journaling became more than just words on a page—it became a refuge, a source of strength, and a way to navigate the uncertainties of life.

Journaling has been one of the most effective tools in my life for adapting and advancing. After losing my father, I began exchanging letters with one of his friends during high school. Those letters became a lifeline—a way for me to process my grief, organize my thoughts, and find direction.

Over the years, journaling has evolved into a daily practice. Each morning, I dedicate two pages to capturing my thoughts, recording Bible verses, noting Thanksgiving points, and reflecting on lessons from sermons, podcasts, or books I've read.

Each day, my journaling practice begins with gratitude, as I take a moment to list the things I'm thankful for. I then focus on a Bible verse that speaks to my current situation, allowing it to guide my thoughts and perspective. As I reflect on my day, I jot down insights from sermons, podcasts, or books that have resonated with me. Finally, I pour out my heart through prayer and personal reflection, expressing my challenges, hopes, and emotions. This practice has been a refuge during life's storms, lifting the weight off my heart and helping me recognize God's hand in every situation.

Adapt and Advance:
How Journaling Transforms Challenges

Journaling is more than just putting words on paper—it is a powerful tool for clearing your mind and finding direction. When life feels overwhelming, writing helps you process emotions, unravel confusion, and turn uncertainty into clarity. It also becomes a tangible record of God's faithfulness, a reminder of how far you've come and how He has carried you through difficult times. Flipping through old journal entries, you see the battles you once thought were impossible and the victories that followed, strengthening your trust in Him. Beyond that, journaling builds resilience, giving you a safe space to express frustrations, gratitude, and hope. It anchors you when life feels unsteady, allowing you to release your burdens while embracing growth and renewal.

The Bible itself affirms the power of writing. In Habakkuk 2:2 (Amplified Bible), God commands, "Write the vision and engrave it plainly on [clay] tablets so that the one who reads it will run." This verse highlights the importance of recording your thoughts, dreams, and reflections. Writing brings clarity, focus, and the motivation to take action. When you put your vision into words, it transforms from a fleeting thought into a purpose-driven path forward.

Very Important Next Step

Dedicating just ten minutes daily to journaling your thoughts, Bible verses, and lessons from your day can become a life-changing practice. In moments of uncertainty, writing provides a powerful way to process emotions, and clarify your thoughts. When you document your struggles, prayers, and reflections, you create a tangible record of God's faithfulness. This practice not only helps release burdens but also serves as a reminder of past victories, reinforcing resilience and faith. With each entry, you transform chaos into clarity and setbacks into stepping stones, strengthening your ability to adapt and advance against all odds.

To begin, set aside ten minutes in a quiet space, preferably in the morning or before bed. Use a notebook or digital journal to structure your entries. Start with gratitude—write down one thing you're thankful for. Next, include a Bible verse that speaks to your current situation. Then, reflect on a lesson from your day, whether from a sermon, podcast, or personal experience. Finally, write a short prayer or personal reflection on how you feel and what steps you need to take next. Over time, this simple habit will become a transformative practice, anchoring you in faith and resilience.

Take action today:

- Set aside ten minutes daily.
- Write one Bible verse, one thing you're thankful for, and one lesson from the day.
- Reflect on your emotions and what you've learned.

By making journaling a daily habit, you create a sacred space to release your burdens, embrace gratitude, and gain clarity. Even in the darkest moments, your words will serve as a beacon of hope, guiding you forward with faith and strength.

Worksheet or Exercise for Growth

1. Gratitude Journal: Write down three things you're thankful for today.

2. Bible Verse Reflection: Choose a verse that speaks to you and write about how it applies to your life.

3. Plan of Action: Identify one challenge you're facing and list one step you can take to address it.

Journaling is a powerful tool for spiritual and emotional growth.

Let your journal be a safe space for reflection, gratitude, and prayer.

Journaling is more than just writing; it's a lifeline for navigating life's challenges. By putting your thoughts on paper, you create space for clarity, gratitude, and growth. Next, we'll explore how bold, periodic transitions—rooted in God's Word—can guide you toward adapting and advancing through life's uncertainties.

SECTION 2
ACTION

This section describes a journey of transformation and perseverance, consisting of four chapters that provide insights and practical tools for overcoming challenges, defying limits, and cultivating resilience in the face of adversity.

It begins with Chapter 8, *Take Bold and Massive Actions*, which emphasizes the importance of taking bold steps to achieve your goals. The chapter offers strategies for moving past fear and embracing consistent, massive action, allowing you to break free from hesitation and start making tangible progress toward your dreams. By learning from figures such as Grant Cardone and Oprah Winfrey, you will be encouraged to set lofty goals and take decisive actions to propel yourself forward.

Next, in Chapter 9, *Defying All Odds to Do the Impossible*, we explore the power of resilience and faith in overcoming obstacles that seem insurmountable. With inspiring stories from individuals like Ross Edgley, who swam around Great Britain, and my own experience of defying expectations in the medical field, this chapter teaches you how to break down large challenges into smaller, actionable steps. It's about learning to rise above limitations by staying focused on the vision ahead and pushing through adversity, no matter how daunting the path may seem.

Moving forward, Chapter 10, *Victory Starts Within: Conquering the Battle in Your Mind*, dives deep into the internal struggles that often hold us back from realizing our potential. In this chapter, you'll learn how to master your mindset, confront limiting beliefs, and turn self-doubt into motivation. Drawing inspiration from Michael Jordan's unwavering focus and the wisdom of spiritual teachings, this chapter provides actionable steps to help you cultivate a victorious mindset, eliminate distractions, and overcome the internal battles that stand in your way. By doing so, you'll unlock your true potential and achieve success, both internally and externally.

Finally, Chapter 11, *Small Steps, Big Impact: Overcoming Mental Health Challenges in Tough Times*, illustrates the power of small, consistent actions in improving mental health and building emotional resilience. This chapter highlights how even the smallest positive habits—such as practicing gratitude, engaging in physical activity, and fostering meaningful connections—can lead to lasting change. With examples from Alex Korb's personal journey and my own story of perseverance through grief, you'll learn how to take daily steps toward emotional health and well-being. By committing to these small actions, you will create a powerful upward spiral that transforms your mental state, even in the most challenging times.

CHAPTER 8

Take Bold and Massive Actions.

W hy did the procrastinator finally take action? Because they realized their bucket list would be repossessed if they didn't act soon.

It's easy to laugh at procrastination, but in reality, delaying action often leads to missed opportunities and lingering regrets. The difference between those who achieve greatness and those who don't isn't just talent or luck—it's the willingness to take bold steps, even when the path ahead feels uncertain.

How many dreams have you put on hold, waiting for the "perfect moment"? How many ideas have you let fade because fear, doubt, or hesitation got in the way? Life doesn't wait. If you don't take action, opportunities slip through your fingers like sand. Every great success story begins with a single decision—the decision to move forward, even when the path is uncertain. The time to act is now, because your future is built on the steps you take today.

In this chapter, you will learn how to take bold and massive actions that align with your goals. We will explore how to overcome fear, stay focused, commit fully, and prioritize consistent efforts. By the end, you'll be equipped to step out of your comfort zone and pursue greatness. Success isn't reserved for those who simply dream; it belongs to those who take decisive steps toward their goals. As Steve Maraboli reminds us, even the smallest action is more powerful than the grandest intention—because movement, no matter how small, is what propels us forward.

> "Take action. An inch of movement will bring you
> closer to your goals than a mile of intention."
>
> —Steve Maraboli

Taking action is what separates those who dream from those who achieve. No matter how ambitious your goals are, progress only happens when you move beyond intention and step into execution. This principle is evident in the lives of high achievers like Grant Cardone, who built his success by embracing bold, relentless action. His *10X Rule* proves that thinking bigger and acting faster can break limitations and create extraordinary results.

How This Worked for Successful People: Grant Cardone and the 10* Rule

Grant Cardone, a renowned entrepreneur, achieved monumental success by applying seven key principles outlined in his *10X Rule*. These principles emphasize the power of relentless action, consistency, and focus. His philosophy teaches that success isn't just about setting goals—it's about thinking bigger, acting faster, and pushing beyond conventional limits.

1. Set 10X Goals

The foundation of the *10X Rule* is setting goals that are ten times greater than what you initially think is possible. Thinking bigger forces you to rise beyond limitations, cultivating discipline, innovation, and an unstoppable drive.

It's not just about reaching the goal but about who you become in the process. Elon Musk embodies this mindset—his vision to make life multi-planetary through SpaceX is a 10X goal that challenges humanity's limits. Despite countless setbacks, his audacity fuels groundbreaking innovations.

2. Take 10X Action

Massive success demands massive action. Average effort yields average results, but extraordinary achievements come from relentless execution. It requires a level of commitment that most people aren't willing to give. Oprah Winfrey's rise from hosting a small talk show to building a media empire was not by chance—it was the result of relentless work ethic and seizing every opportunity. She outworked her peers and turned her dreams into reality. As Pablo Picasso put it, *"Action is the foundational key to all success."*

3. Overcome Fear

Fear is a paralyzing force that holds back potential, but those who achieve greatness learn to channel it into motivation. Facing fear head-on transforms it into courage and resilience, enabling remarkable achievements. Jeff Bezos had to make a terrifying decision—leaving a stable Wall Street career to pursue an untested idea: e-commerce. His willingness to embrace uncertainty led to the creation of Amazon, one of the most influential companies in history. *"Courage is resistance to fear, mastery of fear—not absence of fear,"* said Mark Twain, reminding us that fear isn't the enemy; inaction is.

4. Focus Relentlessly

Success requires eliminating distractions and directing energy toward a singular, compelling goal. A scattered mind produces scattered results, but those who master focus achieve unparalleled excellence. Serena Williams' unwavering dedication to tennis made her a global sports icon. From rigorous training schedules to mental conditioning, she committed herself fully to mastering her craft, resulting in 23 Grand Slam titles. *"Focus is more important than intelligence,"* says an old adage, emphasizing that deep concentration outperforms raw talent.

5. Commit Fully

Partial commitment leads to mediocre results, but full dedication creates momentum and lasting success. True commitment means aligning every decision and action with your ultimate goal, no matter how challenging the journey. Dwayne "The Rock" Johnson is a prime example. Transitioning from wrestling to Hollywood wasn't easy, but through relentless training, acting classes, and strategic career moves, he transformed himself into one of the highest-paid actors in the world. Peter Drucker said it best: *"Unless commitment is made, there are only promises and hopes...but no plans."*

6. Control Time

Time is the most valuable resource, and successful people master it by prioritizing actions that align with their vision. Managing time efficiently ensures maximum productivity. Steve Jobs exemplified this principle by focusing his energy on creating innovative products at Apple. His ability to prioritize simplicity and excellence reshaped the world of technology. Stephen R. Covey captures this truth: *"The key is in not spending time, but in investing it."*

7. **Accept Responsibility**

Taking responsibility means owning your successes and failures, learning from mistakes, and using them as stepping stones for growth. When you take full accountability, you gain control over your results and refine your strategies for long-term success. Warren Buffett is known for openly admitting his investment mistakes, using them as lessons to improve his decision-making. His transparency builds trust and reinforces his proactive leadership. As Jeff Bezos once said, *"In the end, we are our choices."*

These seven principles reinforce that success isn't accidental—it's intentional. When you dream bigger, take relentless action, overcome fear, focus on your goals, commit fully, master your time, and take responsibility for your outcomes, you create a life of extraordinary achievement. The question is, are you ready to 10X your life?

My Story

Like Warren Buffett, I too had to take full responsibility for my choices, embracing uncertainty and stepping into the unknown. Owning my decisions meant trusting that each bold step, no matter how daunting, would lead to growth and transformation. Like Jeff Bezos, I had to push past fear and take a leap of faith, knowing that I wouldn't succeed if I kept hesitating.

In 2014, as I prepared to leave Nigeria for the U.S., I was overwhelmed with uncertainty and fear. I was walking away from my role as an attending physician to start over as a Ph.D. student, and I had no idea what lay ahead. Was I making the right decision? Would I be able to rebuild everything from scratch?

Then, on June 21st, I felt the Holy Spirit lead me to John 21:6: *"Throw your net on the right side of the boat, and you will find some."* In that moment, peace washed over me. This verse was a divine reassurance that provision was ahead, even if I couldn't see it yet.

Now, a decade later, I can testify to God's unwavering faithfulness. Doors I never imagined have opened, opportunities have flourished, and my family has been sustained in ways only He could orchestrate. Taking that leap of faith—stepping beyond my comfort zone—was the catalyst for countless breakthroughs. Leaving behind stability to pursue a new path required courage, resilience, and an unwavering belief in God's guidance. Looking back, I see that every challenge, every sacrifice, and every moment of doubt was met with God's provision, proving that when we trust Him fully, He never fails.

Adapt and Advance

Stepping out of our comfort zone is often the catalyst for miracles. Whether it's taking bold steps in your career, relationships, or personal growth, true transformation begins when we move beyond fear and embrace faith. It is in these moments of uncertainty that God equips us, providing strength and direction when we align our actions with His purpose.

As Steve Maraboli wisely stated, *"Take action. An inch of movement will bring you closer to your goals than a mile of intention."* This quote serves as a powerful reminder that success doesn't come from waiting for the perfect conditions, but from making progress, one step at a time. Plans and dreams hold no weight without action.

The smallest step forward is more valuable than the grandest intention left unrealized.

John 21:6 (AMP) echoes this truth: *"And He said to them, 'Cast the net on the right-hand side of the boat [and you will find some].' So they cast it, and then they were not able to haul it in because of the great catch of fish."* This verse illustrates the power of obedience and divine guidance. Even when past efforts have yielded no results, trusting in God's direction can lead to extraordinary breakthroughs. When we take bold action in faith, we open ourselves to blessings beyond what we could have imagined.

Very Important Next Step

Bold dreams remain just that—dreams—until action breathes life into them. It's not enough to hope, plan, or wait for the perfect moment; transformation happens when you take decisive steps toward your goals. Each day, commit to identifying one bold action that moves you forward. Write it down, pray over it, seek wisdom from the Bible, and take a step—no matter how small—toward making it a reality.

Taking bold actions is what separates those who succeed from those who remain stuck in endless intention. As seen in the lives of Grant Cardone, Elon Musk, and Oprah Winfrey, success isn't about the size of the dream but the size of the action. Small, consistent steps create momentum, and momentum fuels lasting change. It's not about waiting for the right conditions; it's about moving forward despite uncertainty.

Set aside five minutes each morning to identify a bold action for the day, then ask yourself, *"What can I do today to move closer to my goal?"* Write it down, pray for guidance, and take that first step, trusting that action—no matter how small—will propel you forward. Regularly track your progress, adjust as needed, and stay committed. The time to act is now. Your future is built on the bold decisions you make today.

Worksheet or Exercise for Growth

1. Reflection: Write down one bold goal that seems unattainable today.

2. Action Plan: Break it into small, actionable steps.

3. Accountability: Share your progress with someone you trust weekly.

> "When you realize God's purpose for your life isn't
> just about you, He will use you in a mighty way."
> —Dr. Tony Evans

Taking bold, massive actions paves the way for incredible achievements. In the next chapter, we'll explore how to defy all odds to do the impossible.

CHAPTER 9

Defying All Odds to Do the Impossible

W hy did the snail enter the race against the hare? Everyone laughed, saying, *"You'll never win!"*

The snail smiled and replied, *"I'm not here to win; I'm here to defy the odds."*

Though it didn't cross the finish line first, it proved that persistence, not speed, makes the real difference. The snail's journey is a reminder that success isn't always about winning—it's about showing up, persevering, and proving what's possible. Likewise, in life, the greatest victories often come not from immediate success but from the courage to keep moving forward despite the odds.

How many times have you been told that something is impossible? That you don't have what it takes? That your dreams are too big, too unrealistic? History is filled with people who refused to listen to doubt and chose to defy the odds instead. The question isn't whether challenges will come—they will. The real question is, will you let them define you, or will you rise above them? This chapter will show you how faith, resilience, and purposeful action can help you break through limitations and achieve the impossible.

Defying the odds is a path anyone can take. In this chapter, you will discover how to overcome obstacles, rise above limitations, and achieve what others might consider impossible. You'll learn that faith, resilience, and purposeful action can transform challenges into stepping stones toward your dreams.

The only true limits are the ones we accept or impose upon ourselves. When we choose to push beyond fear and doubt, we unlock possibilities we never thought existed. As Ronald Reagan reminds us, the greatest barriers are not external—they are the ones we create in our own minds.

> "There are no constraints on the human mind, no walls around the human spirit, no barriers to our progress except those we ourselves erect."
>
> —Ronald Reagan

How This Worked for Successful People: Ross Edgley: Swimming Around Great Britain.

Ross Edgley, an award-winning adventurer and best-selling author, became the first person in history to swim 1,780 miles around Great Britain in 2018. This grueling feat took 157 days and required immense physical and mental resilience.

Despite facing arctic storms, jellyfish stings, polluted waters, and physical deterioration so severe his tongue began to disintegrate, Ross persevered. His coach initially labeled the challenge "impossible" due to the sheer distance, relentless currents, and the toll on the human body. However, Ross defied these odds by applying principles of Stoicism, preparation, and mental toughness.

Like Ross, you may face seemingly insurmountable challenges, moments when the odds seem stacked against you. But if you develop resilience, stay committed, and take consistent action, you too can accomplish the impossible. His story reminds us that perseverance, strategic preparation, and mental strength can transform even the toughest obstacles into stepping stones toward success. His story is a testament to the power of resilience and faith in achieving the unthinkable.

My Story

Like Ross Edgley, I too had to confront challenges that seemed overwhelming, moments when others doubted my ability to succeed. Yet, just as he relied on resilience and perseverance to push through, I had to trust in my own determination and faith to keep moving forward. Like him, I faced obstacles that could have easily discouraged me, but instead of giving in to doubt, I chose to believe in God's plan. Through persistence and unwavering faith, I was able to defy expectations and achieve what once seemed impossible.

In high school, I faced a significant hurdle: I had to retake my Chemistry exam to secure a passing grade necessary for medical school admission. During this challenging time, a well-meaning cousin suggested that pursuing a career in medicine might be beyond my capabilities, given its demanding nature. While their advice was practical, it had the potential to deter me from my passion.

Choosing to trust in God's plan, I embarked on my medical journey. In 1997, I gained admission to medical school and, by 2003, I graduated, successfully passing all four major exams on my first attempt. This achievement was just the beginning of a series of milestones that underscored divine guidance in my life.

In 2011, I completed a Residency in Community Medicine and simultaneously earned a master's in public health. My academic pursuits continued, and in 2019, I was awarded a Ph.D. in

Epidemiology. Recognizing the importance of research, I undertook a Postdoctoral Fellowship on an NIH Grant in 2021. Currently, I am progressing through a Psychiatry Residency, with an anticipated completion in 2025.

Each phase of this journey serves as a testament to the belief that when God opens a door, no one can shut it (Isaiah 22:22).

Adapt and Advance

Ross Edgley's journey mirrors my own, reminding me that challenges are opportunities in disguise. God has the final say in our lives, but we must act in faith and work diligently toward the open doors He provides.

As Walt Disney wisely said, "The way to get started is to quit talking and begin doing." This quote teaches us that making progress is less about thinking than it is about doing. Take that first step toward your dream today. Martin Luther King Jr. further emphasized that "Human progress is neither automatic nor inevitable. Every step toward the goals requires sacrifice, suffering, and struggle." This reminds us that achieving our goals demands effort and perseverance. C.S. Lewis captures the essence of resilience perfectly: "Progress means getting nearer to the place you want to be. If you have taken a wrong turn, progress means doing an about-turn and walking back to the right road." This highlights that recognizing and correcting our mistakes is essential for true progress.

Success begins with a clear vision. Obstacles and limitations often appear overwhelming because they obscure the end goal. By having an unshakable vision, you maintain focus on the big picture, which fuels perseverance during tough times. A powerful vision serves as a compass, guiding you even when the path seems uncertain. Sara Blakely's journey to becoming the youngest self-made billionaire began with an idea: creating comfortable, slimming undergarments for women. Despite having no background in fashion, manufacturing, or business, her vision was crystal clear. Despite facing repeated rejections from manufacturers and investors, she pressed on, developing prototypes and cold-calling hosiery mills.

Her determination eventually paid off when Neiman Marcus agreed to stock her products. Today, Spanx is a global brand, underscoring the power of holding onto your vision despite industry rejection or lack of resources. When you stick to your vision, obstacles become stepping stones.

Obstacles often provide valuable lessons when approached with the right mindset. Instead of viewing setbacks as failures, see them as opportunities to improve, innovate, or pivot. This resilience helps you push past limitations and achieve seemingly impossible goals. Howard Schultz, CEO of Starbucks, grew up in a poor housing complex in Brooklyn, New York. When he first encountered a small coffee shop called Starbucks, he envisioned transforming it into an international chain focused on creating a coffeehouse experience. However, Schultz's initial proposal to expand Starbucks was rejected by its owners. Instead of giving up, he launched his own coffee business, Il Giornale, and eventually bought Starbucks outright. Schultz's setbacks taught him to adapt and innovate, including introducing the Starbucks rewards program and café culture to the U.S. market. His ability to learn from rejection and failure propelled Starbucks to become a global brand, and shows us that turning setbacks into learning moments can provide the insight needed to surpass obstacles.

Success is often a team sport. Recognize your unique strengths and supplement your weaknesses by building relationships and leveraging the expertise of others. No one achieves the impossible in isolation; collaboration is key. Richard Branson, founder of Virgin Group, has dyslexia, which makes academics challenging. Instead of seeing his dyslexia as a limitation, he used it as a strength by fostering creativity and relying on strong interpersonal skills.

Branson's unique ability to connect with people allowed him to attract talented collaborators and investors. By building a robust network, he launched Virgin Records and later expanded into various industries, from airlines to telecommunications. Branson's empire would not exist if he didn't leverage his strengths and surround himself with a capable team. This example shows that overcoming limitations often requires collaboration and understanding that your quirks are actually your perks.

By cultivating a vision, turning setbacks into opportunities, and leveraging your strengths and networks, you can overcome obstacles, rise above limitations, and achieve what others deem impossible. These principles are exemplified by figures like Sara Blakely, Howard Schultz, and Richard Branson, whose stories remind us that persistence, resilience, and collaboration are the keys to extraordinary success.

Isaiah 22:22 (AMP) states: "Then I will set on his shoulder the key of the house of David; When he opens no one will shut, When he shuts no one will open." This verse highlights God's sovereignty and authority over our lives. Trusting His timing and guidance transforms obstacles into opportunities and empowers us to achieve what seems impossible.

Very Important Next Step

Obstacles can often feel overwhelming, casting doubt on our ability to move forward. However, the key to overcoming even the most insurmountable challenges lies in taking small, intentional steps each day. Instead of allowing obstacles to petrify you, break them down into manageable tasks and commit to tackling them one by one. Each small step builds momentum, turning what once seemed impossible into an achievable reality. This practice not only pushes you beyond your limitations but also makes you more resilient, shaping you into someone who refuses to be defined by adversity.

As seen in Ross Edgley's incredible feat of swimming around Great Britain and my own journey through medical school, perseverance, purposeful action, and faith in God's guidance are essential for overcoming obstacles. Success isn't about finding and following an easy path—it's about pushing forward despite the difficulties, trusting that each step brings you closer to victory.

To put this into action, set aside 5-10 minutes to identify the major obstacles you are facing. Write them down and break each one into smaller, actionable steps. If a daunting project feels overwhelming, divide it into tasks like research, creating an outline, or setting mini deadlines. Each day, choose one specific step to focus on and take consistent action toward completing it. Track your progress and reflect on your growth along the way. This strategic approach— mirroring those of leaders like Howard Schultz and Richard Branson—will help you transform setbacks into stepping stones and steadily move toward success.

Start today: Make a list of three obstacles standing between you and your long-term goals. Develop a clear plan for each and break them into small, daily steps. Most importantly, take consistent action. Progress is built one step at a time, and with faith, persistence, and determination, you will rise above the challenges before you.

Worksheet or Exercise for Growth

1. Reflection: Write down three odds stacked against you.

2. Plan: For each, outline one actionable plan to defy them.

3. Commitment: Take one step toward overcoming these odds today.

4. Accountability: Track your progress weekly and share it with a trusted friend or mentor.

Faith and action go hand in hand.

Progress often starts with small, consistent steps.

Trust God's timing and guidance to overcome the impossible.

In this chapter, we've explored how faith and resilience can help us overcome even the greatest challenges. Up next, we'll uncover strategies to conquer the greatest battlefield of all—the mind—in "Victory Starts Within: Conquering the Battle in Your Mind."

CHAPTER 10

Victory Starts Within: Conquering the Battle in Your Mind.

Why did the brain go to the gym? To flex its muscles and conquer self-doubt.

Just as our bodies need exercise to stay fit, our minds require training to overcome internal challenges. Strengthening mental resilience is essential to achieving personal growth and success.

Imagine your mind as a battlefield where self-doubt and fear wage war against your aspirations. The true victory lies not in external achievements but in mastering this internal struggle. This chapter delves into strategies to strengthen your mental resilience, transform negative thoughts, and emerge triumphant in life's challenges

Just as the brain strengthens through physical exercise, our minds require deliberate effort to overcome internal challenges. By focusing on mental resilience and adopting positive self-talk, we can transform self-doubt into confidence. This chapter delves into strategies to strengthen your mental resilience, transform negative thoughts, and emerge triumphant in life's challenges. To effectively navigate these internal battles, we must first understand the power of our mindset. By doing so, we can learn how we can transform challenges into opportunities for growth.

This chapter delves into strategies to strengthen your mental resilience, transform negative thoughts, and emerge triumphant in life's challenges. In this chapter, we examine the transformative power of mastering your mindset to conquer internal battles and achieve victory in life. You'll discover how to cultivate a mindset that refuses to settle, trust your instincts instead of overthinking, and channel pressure and challenges as fuel for growth. Additionally, we'll explore strategies to eliminate distractions, focus relentlessly, and take ownership of your mental landscape.

To master your mindset and conquer internal battles, it's essential to recognize the power you hold over your own thoughts. As Marcus Aurelius wisely stated, "You have power over your mind—not outside events. Realize this, and you will find strength."

This profound insight underscores the importance of mastering one's internal world to navigate external challenges effectively. Embracing this philosophy, Michael Jordan exemplified how controlling one's mindset effectively can lead to unparalleled success.

How This Worked for Successful People: Michael Jordan

Michael Jordan's relentless mindset exemplifies the principles of conquering internal battles. After being cut from his high school basketball team, he trained obsessively, proving critics wrong and becoming a basketball legend. Jordan channeled personal slights—such as being overlooked in the NBA Draft—into motivation to dominate his peers. In the iconic "Flu Game" during the 1997 NBA Finals, he trusted his preparation and instincts to deliver an unforgettable performance despite being physically exhausted.

Jordan thrived under high-pressure moments, like his game-winning shot against Cleveland in the 1989 playoffs. Known for his laser focus, he demanded excellence from himself and his teammates, cutting out anything that detracted from his goals. After setbacks, Jordan intensified his training, taking full responsibility for his growth. Even after three championships, he returned from retirement to achieve another three-peat, cementing his legacy.

Like Michael Jordan, you may face setbacks that challenge your resolve. However, if you turn these challenges into motivation and maintain relentless focus, you too can achieve the extraordinary. Jordan's journey teaches us that embracing adversity and taking full responsibility for our growth can transform obstacles into stepping stones toward success.

My Story

Like Michael Jordan, I too faced a pivotal setback that tested my resolve and determination. In 2018, I encountered a significant hurdle: failing the United States Medical Licensing Examination (USMLE) Step 1—a critical exam assessing a medical student's grasp of foundational sciences essential for practicing medicine in the U.S. This eight-hour, computer-based test evaluates knowledge in areas such as anatomy, biochemistry, and physiology, and is a critical milestone for medical licensure. At 15 years post-graduation, juggling a demanding life, I doubted my ability to succeed. Initially, I considered quitting, but my children reminded me of the principles I had always instilled in them: "Never give up." This prompted a shift in my mindset; I confronted my self-doubt head-on and, with renewed determination, passed the exam on my second attempt. This victory not only reinstated my confidence but also opened doors to further successes, underscoring that the true battle begins in the mind.

Facing the failure of the USMLE Step One exam was a profound emotional blow. The weight of this setback, especially after years away from formal education, was almost overwhelming. However, this experience became a turning point, reinforcing the belief that true victory begins within the mind. It taught me that setbacks are not the end but a call to adapt, advance, and persist with unwavering faith.

Adapt and Advance

Victory in life requires persistence, focus, and faith. Whether it's passing challenging exams, overcoming financial struggles, or achieving personal milestones, every triumph begins by conquering internal battles. Henry Ford once said, "Whether you think you can or think you can't, you're right." This emphasizes that our mindset plays a pivotal role in overcoming challenges. Believing in our ability to succeed often determines the outcome. Similarly, René Descartes stated, "Conquer yourself rather than the world," highlighting that mastering our internal struggles shapes how we face external challenges.

To navigate these challenges, consider these actions:

1. **Renew Your Mind with God's Word**: Engaging consistently with Scripture helps replace negative thoughts with God's promises of hope and victory. Pastor Rick Warren, author of "The Purpose-Driven Life," overcame doubt and depression by immersing himself in biblical truths, leading to a transformative impact on his life and ministry.

2. **Take Every Thought Captive**: The Bible instructs us to "take captive every thought to make it obedient to Christ" (2 Corinthians 10:5). This involves identifying and rejecting harmful thoughts before they take root.

C.S. Lewis, renowned author of "Mere Christianity," battled skepticism and personal grief, but by challenging his doubts, he transformed his struggles into profound writings that continue to inspire.

3. **Develop a Thankful Attitude**: Gratitude shifts our focus from what we lack to what we have, strengthening mental resilience. Corrie ten Boom, author of "The Hiding Place," maintained a thankful heart even in a Nazi concentration camp, finding reasons to be grateful, which transformed her trials into a legacy of faith and hope.

As 2 Corinthians 10:4-5 reminds us, our battles are spiritual and mental. Aligning our thoughts with God's truth and demolishing anything that opposes it leads to true victory. By renewing our minds, capturing negative thoughts, and cultivating gratitude, we can adapt to challenges and advance toward the life God intends for us.

Very Important Next Step

Your mindset plays a pivotal role in navigating life's challenges. As exemplified by Michael Jordan's relentless positivity and Joyce Meyer's teachings on renewing the mind, confronting negative thoughts and replacing them with empowering beliefs can transform obstacles into opportunities. This practice aligns your thoughts with truth, turning limiting beliefs into catalysts for growth.

To implement this, begin each day by identifying a limiting belief or negative thought you've been battling. Then, select a corresponding Bible verse or positive affirmation that counters it. For instance, if you struggle with self-doubt, reflect on Philippians

4:13: "I can do all things through Christ who strengthens me." Write this empowering truth down, recite it aloud, and focus on it throughout your day. By consistently practicing this exercise, you take control of your thoughts, and prime your mindset primed for victory and resilience.

Remember, each day presents a new opportunity to renew your mind and align your thoughts with empowering truths. Embrace this practice diligently, and witness the transformation in how you approach and overcome life's challenges.

Worksheet or Exercise for Growth

1. Morning Affirmations: Write down three empowering thoughts or Bible verses to start your day.

2. Battle Plan: Identify one mental obstacle you're currently facing. Write an actionable step to overcome it.

3. Gratitude Journal: List three things you're grateful for each evening to train your mind to focus on positivity.

Building mental strength is a daily commitment. Stay consistent, and over time, you'll see transformation in every area of your life. Let's keep adapting and advancing!

True victory begins within—by mastering the mind, embracing challenges, and focusing relentlessly on growth. Now, we move to the next chapter, "Small Steps, Big Impact: Overcoming Mental Health Challenges in Tough Times," where we'll explore how consistent, small actions can lead to lasting transformation.

CHAPTER 11

Small Steps, Big Impact: Overcoming Mental Health Challenges in Tough Times

W hy did the overwhelmed brain break up with procrastination? Because it chose to "take things step by step" and realized procrastination wasn't on board with small, actionable goals.

Recognizing that procrastination hindered its progress, the brain decided to embrace "Baby Steps," starting with simple tasks like making the bed, which led to a sense of accomplishment and momentum. This chapter explores how minor, consistent actions can lead to significant improvements in mental health, offering practical strategies to help you navigate tough times and build resilience

In life's most challenging moments, the path to mental well-being often begins with the smallest steps. This chapter explores how minor, consistent actions can lead to significant improvements in mental health, offering practical strategies to help you navigate tough times and build resilience.

In this chapter, we delve into how small, consistent actions can help you navigate tough times and enhance your mental health.

You'll discover seven powerful strategies to create positive changes in your life, understand how daily steps can lead to transformative results, and gain practical tools to build resilience and move forward, even during the most challenging seasons

Even the smallest actions can set the stage for significant transformation, proving that progress is built step by step. Taking that first step, no matter how small, is often the key to unlocking greater momentum, as reflected in the wisdom of Martin Luther King Jr

"You don't have to see the whole staircase, just take the first step."
– Martin Luther King Jr.

Just as Martin Luther King Jr. emphasized the importance of initiating action, Alex Korb's experience demonstrates how small steps can lead to significant improvements in mental health.

How This Worked for Successful People: Alex Korb

In his book *The Upward Spiral*, neuroscientist Alex Korb shares a deeply personal account of how small, intentional actions became his lifeline during a period of profound despair. During his college years, Korb grappled with intense anxiety and depression. The culmination of these struggles occurred when his girlfriend ended their relationship during a particularly bleak winter, leaving him feeling as though his world was unraveling.

Unbeknownst to him at the time, it was the modest, seemingly trivial habits he maintained that anchored him amidst the turmoil. Engaging in sports subtly elevated his dopamine levels, offering brief yet essential lifts in his mood. Exposure to natural sunlight played a crucial role in regulating his serotonin production, which in turn enhanced his sleep quality and stabilized his emotions. Moreover, the consistent support from friendships provided him with daily doses of emotional connection and reassurance.

These unconscious lifelines, though minor in isolation, collectively wove a safety net that prevented him from descending further into darkness. Korb's experience illuminates a powerful truth: small steps, when practiced consistently, can set in motion a transformative upward spiral, guiding one toward emotional well-being and resilience.

Like Alex Korb, you may face periods of profound despair and emotional turmoil. However, by incorporating small, positive habits into your daily routine, you too can initiate an upward spiral toward emotional well-being. Korb's journey demonstrates that even modest changes can collectively create a powerful foundation for resilience and recovery.

My Story

Like Alex Korb, I too faced moments of profound despair that tested my resilience. During medical school, the weight of losing both parents left me feeling utterly defeated. Observing my peers thrive while I grappled with basic needs deepened my sense of isolation. However, by embracing small, consistent actions—such as practicing gratitude, engaging in regular exercise, fostering meaningful connections, and immersing myself in self-help literature—I gradually transformed my mental well-being. These modest habits became the foundation of my healing journey, illustrating that even in our darkest times, incremental steps can lead to profound change

Adapt and Advance

In life's journey, it's often the small, consistent actions that lead us out of despair and into hope. Practicing gratitude, for instance, shifts our focus from what's lacking to the abundance we possess, fostering a positive outlook even in challenging times.

Engaging in regular physical activity not only strengthens the body but also invigorates the mind, providing clarity and reducing stress. Prioritizing adequate sleep restores our energy and sharpens our mental faculties, enabling us to face each day with renewed vigor. Making intentional daily decisions, no matter how minor they seem, empowers us to take control of our lives and steer them in the desired direction.

Building meaningful connections offers a support system, reminding us that we are not alone in our struggles. Embracing small, consistent changes allows us to build momentum, leading to significant transformations over time. Feeding our minds with self-help resources equips us with tools and insights to navigate life's challenges more effectively.

The Bible underscores the importance of these practices. 1 Thessalonians 5:18 encourages us to "Give thanks in all circumstances; for this is God's will for you in Christ Jesus." This verse reminds us that gratitude is a powerful tool, even in adversity. 1 Corinthians 6:19 emphasizes the sanctity of our bodies: "Do you not know that your bodies are temples of the Holy Spirit?" This calls us to honor our physical well-being.

Proverbs 3:24 speaks to the value of rest: "When you lie down, you will not be afraid; when you lie down, your sleep will be sweet." This assures us of the peace that comes with trusting in God's protection. Proverbs 16:3 advises, "Commit to the Lord whatever you do, and he will establish your plans," highlighting the importance of intentionality in our actions.

Proverbs 27:17 states, "As iron sharpens iron, so one person sharpens another," emphasizing the role of community in personal growth. Luke 16:10 reminds us, "Whoever can be trusted with very little can also be trusted with much," encouraging faithfulness in small steps. Proverbs 18:15 notes, "The heart of the discerning acquires knowledge, for the ears of the wise seek it out," urging us to continually seek wisdom and understanding.

By integrating these habits into our daily routines, we align ourselves with a path of resilience and growth. Each small step, grounded in faith and intentionality, propels us forward, transforming challenges into opportunities and leading us toward the abundant life that God envisions for us

Very Important Next Step

Taking small, intentional actions every day can be the key to overcoming challenges and improving mental health. To put this into practice, start by identifying three strategies from the list of seven habits and dedicate at least five minutes to each, totaling just 15 minutes daily. Though these actions may seem small, their impact can be profound, helping you build resilience, gain clarity, and create a sense of emotional well-being.

Small, consistent steps are often the most powerful tools for transformation. Whether it's practicing gratitude, engaging in physical activity, or simply making a mindful choice each day, these habits accumulate, creating a positive cycle of growth. Just like in Alex Korb's story, where simple actions helped shift his mental state and led him toward healing, these small efforts can also guide you toward emotional strength. By committing to these daily actions, you align yourself with steady progress, no matter how difficult the journey may seem.

To make this a reality, begin by writing down three strategies you want to implement. It could be as simple as journaling one thing you're grateful for, taking a 10-minute walk, or reading a chapter from a self-help book. Set aside a specific time each day to engage in these habits and use a notebook or digital app to track your progress. Celebrate the small victories, because each step forward, no matter how minor, is a step toward healing, growth, and lasting change.

Every day, pick one habit from the list and practice it for five minutes. Gradually incorporate more habits as they become part of your routine.

Worksheet or Exercise for Growth

1. Morning Gratitude: List three things you're grateful for.

2. Daily Movement: Commit to ten minutes of physical activity.

3. Intentional Connection: Reach out to one person who uplifts you and strengthens that relationship.

Small, consistent actions lead to significant transformations. No matter where you start, trust the process and keep moving forward—step by step.

Small steps have the power to create lasting change, even during life's most challenging times. As we continue this journey, we'll explore how discovering God's plan for your life provides clarity, purpose, and hope. Get ready to unlock divine guidance and step into your calling!

SECTION 3
PLANNING

This section describes the journey of discovering, planning, and executing God's purpose in your life. It consists of three chapters that build on the foundational principles of faith, resilience, and intentional action. The chapters guide you through the steps of identifying and aligning with God's plan, creating clear and actionable goals, and learning to overcome obstacles with unwavering confidence. Through these principles, you will be empowered to take bold actions, plan effectively, and embrace life's challenges as opportunities for growth.

In Chapter 12, Discover God's Plan for Your Life, you will begin a transformative journey toward discovering God's plan for your life, which is not only good but designed with purpose. Often, we may feel lost or uncertain about our direction, especially during challenging seasons. However, the truth remains that God has intricately woven each of us for a specific purpose. Understanding and aligning with God's plan requires not only faith and reflection but also small, intentional steps every day.

Through this chapter, you will learn to embrace your God-given talents, passions, and opportunities, drawing closer to your divine calling. We'll explore how you can identify the goals that resonate with your heart, ensuring that they align with God's Word and purpose. You will also be encouraged to start with small steps that transform what may feel like an overwhelming journey into achievable and purposeful actions. As Rick Warren's teachings remind us, life begins to make sense when you align with God's purpose, as you see His guidance unfold with every decision.

In Chapter 13, "Planning with CCOPS: Capture, Clarify, Organize, Prioritize, Simplify", with the clarity of God's plan in mind, the next crucial step is effective planning. Often, our dreams and goals feel impossible because we lack the clarity or structure to bring them to fruition. This chapter will introduce the CCOPS framework, and show you how this systematic approach can structure your daily life for maximum impact, while also helping you to break down large, overwhelming tasks into manageable actions.

By learning to capture every thought and idea, clarify its purpose, organize it into categories, prioritize it based on importance, and simplify it into clear, actionable steps, you will build a strong foundation for pursuing your goals. As Abraham Lincoln once said, "Give me six hours to chop down a tree, and I will spend the first four sharpening the axe." This quote highlights the importance of preparation, and CCOPS serves as the tool that sharpens your planning, ensuring that every action you take is focused and purposeful.

In Chapter 14, "Plan B: The Obstacle in Your Plan Is the Road to Greatness," you will learn that while planning is essential, it is equally important to remain flexible and resilient when obstacles arise. Life rarely goes as planned, and the key to success often lies in how we adapt to and overcome challenges. In this chapter, you will learn how to embrace setbacks as opportunities to recalibrate and move forward with even greater strength.

Through stories of success, such as John D. Rockefeller's ability to turn obstacles into opportunities and my personal journey of perseverance through academic challenges, you will see how flexibility and faith work hand-in-hand to help you grow. The obstacles in your life are not roadblocks; rather, they are redirections that teach you important lessons. By creating backup plans (Plan B, C, and D) and staying resilient, you'll be empowered to press forward in the face of adversity. With God's guidance, each setback can be transformed into a stepping stone toward greater success and fulfillment.

CHAPTER 12

Discover God's Plan for Your Life.

A man prayed fervently, asking God to reveal His plan for his life. Suddenly, the clouds parted, and a booming voice said, "You are going to help the world by serving others!" Excited, the man asked, "That's amazing! But Lord, could you be more specific?" The voice replied, "Start by doing the dishes. Your wife has been praying, too!"

Embarking on the journey to discover God's purpose often begins with simple, everyday actions. Before we explore the actionable faithful steps, this chapter will spur us to reflect on what God's plan might look like in your life, and how small actions can align with His greater purpose.

In this chapter, we'll explore how aligning with His plan involves embracing humility, serving others, and finding significance in the mundane. Uncover how these small steps can lead to profound fulfillment and clarity in your divine calling. Sometimes God's plan starts with the small, faithful steps we tend to overlook! God's plan for your life is good, purposeful, and achievable. By the end of this chapter, you'll have clarity on how to align with His plan, understand key principles, and identify daily steps to walk in it.

Understanding that our lives are designed by and for God is essential to finding true meaning and purpose. As Rick Warren insightfully points out, without this divine perspective, life remains perplexing and unfulfilled. Similarly, Louie Giglio emphasizes that God's plans for us transcend our immediate circumstances, offering a hope and future beyond our present understanding.

How this worked for successful people: Rick Warren

Rick Warren's journey as a pastor, author, and global leader is an excellent example of discovering and living God's plan. His book The Purpose Driven Life has sold over 50 million copies and changed countless lives.

Rick Warren's life exemplifies the five biblical purposes he outlines in *The Purpose Driven Life*, demonstrating their transformative impact when applied with intention.

1. Worship: Bringing Glory to God

Warren emphasizes that worship involves centering one's life around God, extending beyond traditional practices to a lifestyle that honors Him in all aspects. In his own journey, Warren dedicated his talents and resources to God's service, notably through the success of his book. He and his wife, Kay, made the decision to "reverse tithe," giving away 90 percent of their income and living on the remaining ten percent. This act of generosity reflects a profound commitment to glorify God with their blessings, showcasing worship through stewardship and trust.

2. Fellowship: Building Relationships with Believers

Understanding the importance of community, Warren fostered deep connections within his church and the global Christian community. He initiated small group networks within Saddleback

Church, creating environments where members could support and encourage one another. This emphasis on fellowship has cultivated a sense of belonging and mutual growth, reinforcing the idea that spiritual development flourishes in the context of authentic relationships.

3. Discipleship: Growing Spiritually

Warren's commitment to discipleship is evident in his dedication to studying and teaching God's Word. He pursued theological education and applied biblical principles to his life and ministry. By sharing his insights through sermons, books, and training programs, Warren has guided countless individuals toward spiritual maturity, demonstrating that continuous learning and application of Scripture are vital for personal and communal transformation.

4. Ministry: Serving Others

Recognizing that serving others is central to God's purpose, Warren has utilized his unique gifts to address global issues. He launched the P.E.A.C.E. Plan, a worldwide initiative aimed at combating problems like poverty, disease, and illiteracy. This endeavor mobilizes local churches to serve their communities, reflecting Warren's belief that every individual has a role in ministering to others. His leadership in this area underscores the impact of aligning one's talents with service, resulting in meaningful change.

5. Mission: Sharing God's Love Globally

Warren's sense of mission extends beyond his local congregation. He has been actively involved in global evangelism, partnering with leaders and churches worldwide to spread the message of Christ. His work in Rwanda, for instance, has contributed to national efforts toward reconciliation and development. By sharing God's love on a global scale, Warren exemplifies the calling to participate in the Great Commission, inspiring others to embrace their role in this divine mandate.

Through these lived experiences, Rick Warren demonstrates that embracing these five purposes leads to a life of significance and fulfillment, which aligns with God's overarching plan.

My Story

Embarking on my PhD journey, I set an ambitious goal: achieving a perfect 4.0 GPA. This aspiration, inspired by Hebrews 10:38—"And my righteous ones will live by faith..."—was not just a personal milestone but a testament to glorify God. However, the path was fraught with challenges. The weight of this seemingly unattainable goal often filled me with fear and self-doubt. I questioned my capabilities, wondering if I had set myself up for failure.

Each course presented its own set of obstacles, and there were moments when the pressure felt overwhelming. Yet, in these times of uncertainty, I leaned heavily on my faith, trusting that God would provide the strength and guidance I needed. Through unwavering perseverance, countless hours of study, and a steadfast reliance on divine support, I navigated the ups and downs of the program. While I didn't achieve the perfect 4.0, earning a final GPA of 3.9 became a profound testament to God's faithfulness and grace. This journey taught me that even when our aspirations seem beyond reach, with faith and determination, we can accomplish remarkable feats.

Throughout this journey, I dedicated my academic success to glorifying God, ensuring that my studies were an act of worship. I remained connected to my church family at Newspring Church, actively participating in fellowship and service. Regular Bible study and prayer shaped my confidence and decisions, deepening my discipleship. I served middle and high school students, guiding new believers in their faith journeys, fulfilling my ministerial purpose. Additionally, I volunteered with care teams, sharing God's love with those in need, embracing my mission. This journey wasn't without challenges, but by aligning with God's plan, I emerged stronger and closer to Him.

In addition to engaging in these spiritual practices, I maintained a rigorous study schedule, attended all classes, prepared diligently for exams, and submitted assignments promptly. I recognized that faith must be accompanied by action, as emphasized in James 2:18: "But someone may say, 'You [claim to] have faith and I have [good] works; show me your [alleged] faith without the works [if you can], and I will show you my faith by my works [that is, by what I do]."

Adapt and Advance

My journey towards a 3.9 GPA in my PhD program was fraught with challenges that tested my resolve and faith. To navigate this demanding path, I employed several strategies that not only bolstered my academic performance but also deepened my spiritual connection.

Mastering time management was paramount. By utilizing planners and setting clear priorities, I ensured that each task was addressed promptly, aligning with the biblical principle of making the best use of time as emphasized in Ephesians 5:15-16: "Look carefully then how you walk, not as unwise but as wise, making the best use of the time, because the days are evil."

Delving deeply into my studies, I sought to understand concepts beyond their surface meanings. This dedication mirrors the call in Proverbs 4:7: "The beginning of wisdom is this: Get wisdom.

Though it costs all you have, get understanding." Building meaningful relationships with my professors provided guidance and mentorship, reflecting the wisdom of Proverbs 11:14: "Where there is no guidance, a people falls, but in an abundance of counselors there is safety."

Developing effective study techniques, such as active recall and spaced repetition, enhanced my retention of complex material. Collaborating with peers through study groups fostered a supportive learning environment, embodying the essence of Proverbs 27:17: "As iron sharpens iron, so one person sharpens another." Maintaining consistency by breaking down large tasks into manageable steps kept me disciplined and focused.

Balancing academic demands with physical well-being was crucial. Regular exercise, adequate sleep, and stress management not only rejuvenated my body but also honored the truth found in 1 Corinthians 6:19: "Do you not know that your bodies are temples of the Holy Spirit?" These combined efforts not only propelled me toward academic excellence but also drew me closer to God, teaching me to trust Him in every facet of my life.

Identifying God's plan for one's life involves intentional and heartfelt practices. Seeking God through prayer and immersion in His Word is foundational. As James 1:5 encourages: "If any of you lacks wisdom, let him ask God, who gives generously to all without reproach, and it will be given him." By dedicating time daily to converse with God and meditate on scriptures, we open our hearts to His guidance, allowing His Word to illuminate our path as stated in Psalm 119:105: "Your word is a lamp to my feet and a light to my path."

Recognizing our passions and gifts is another avenue through which God reveals His purpose. Reflecting on activities that bring joy and fulfillment can provide insights into our divine calling. Romans 12:6-8 speaks to this: "We have different gifts, according to the grace given to each of us..." Engaging in what we are passionate about not only brings personal satisfaction but also serves others, aligning with God's plan.

Observing open doors and divine opportunities requires a heart attuned to God's movements in our lives. Proverbs 3:5-6 advises: "Trust in the Lord with all your heart and lean not on your own understanding; in all your ways submit to him, and he will make your paths straight." By trusting in Him and remaining attentive to the opportunities He presents, we can discern His will and direction for our lives.

Reflecting on the wisdom of spiritual leaders can further inspire and guide us. Rick Warren once said, "You were made by God and for God, and until you understand that, life will never make sense." Louie Giglio also reminds us, "God's plans for your life far exceed the circumstances of your day." These insights emphasize that aligning with God's will and trusting Him through every season is essential for a purposeful and fulfilling life.

In embracing these principles, we can adapt to life's challenges and advance toward the destiny God has ordained for us, finding strength, purpose, and joy in His unwavering presence.

Very Important Next Step

Embarking on a journey aligned with God's purpose begins with intentional goal setting. Setting well-defined goals provides clarity and direction, ensuring your actions are purpose-driven and aligned with God's greater vision for your life. Breaking down large goals into smaller, manageable tasks transforms the seemingly impossible into attainable milestones. As Pastor Rick

Warren emphasizes, fulfilling God's purposes involves taking intentional steps that draw you closer to your divine assignment.

To implement this, begin by spending time in prayer and meditation, seeking God's guidance to reveal the three most important goals you are meant to achieve in your lifetime. Write each one down, ensuring they align with your faith and divine purpose. For each goal, delineate specific actions required annually, monthly, weekly, and daily. For instance, if spiritual growth is a goal, daily Bible reading and prayer could be part of your routine. Affirm each action with relevant Scripture, grounding your steps in God's Word. Dedicate yourself to these tasks, trusting in God's strength to guide you. Regularly review and adjust your plans as needed, remaining open to His direction and timing. Celebrate small victories along the way, acknowledging God's hand in your progress.

The benefit of this structured approach is that not only fosters progress but also deepens your relationship with God. By faithfully undertaking these steps, you actively participate in the realization of God's plan for your life, experiencing the profound fulfillment that comes from walking in harmony with His will.

Worksheet or Exercise for Growth

1. Write three lifetime goals.

2. Break each goal into annual, monthly, weekly, and daily actionable steps.

3. Reflect: Do these plans align with your mission and God's purpose?

4. Identify one daily habit to keep you aligned with each goal.

God's plan for your life may unfold one step at a time, but faithfulness in small actions leads to greater clarity and purpose. Trust Him in every moment.

By now, you've gained clarity on God's overarching plan for your life and identified actionable steps to align with it. In the next chapter, we'll focus on breaking these plans into simple, actionable steps: Capture. Clarify. Organize. Prioritize. Simplify to Actionable Steps.

CHAPTER 13

Planning with CCOPS: Capture, Clarify, Organize, Prioritize, Simplify

I tried to plan my week without using CCOPS. Monday vanished, Tuesday exploded, Wednesday filed a complaint, and by Thursday, my to-do list just laughed and walked away. Now I Capture, Clarify, Organize, Prioritize, and Simplify—because even my coffee needed a strategy meeting!

Imagine the moment when disorder gives way to focus through one powerful decision. In this chapter, you'll discover how a clear, deliberate planning approach transforms your loftiest dreams into a series of achievable steps. Rather than seeking shortcuts, each intentional action breaks down barriers and sparks creativity, guiding you on an unmistakable path to success.

Now that we understand the importance of making intentional decisions, it's time to explore a framework for turning vision into reality. With the right tools and approach, you can bring structure to your goals and confidently take actionable steps toward success. A spark of purposeful organization ignites a method that reshapes unruly ambitions into tangible daily wins. Now, adopt a structure that transforms scattered ideas into a definitive roadmap, propelling you confidently toward your next milestone.

In this chapter, you will learn how to use the CCOPS framework— Capture, Clarify, Organize, Prioritize, Simplify to Actionable Steps—to structure your daily tasks effectively. By applying these principles, you will transform overwhelming goals into manageable actions, allowing you to achieve your dreams with clarity and purpose.

Effective planning is the key to turning challenges into achievements, ensuring each step is purposeful. By doing this, you build a bridge between your vast ambitions and clear, targeted daily actions.

How This Worked for Successful People: David Allen, the author of Getting Things Done

David Allen, the mastermind behind *Getting Things Done: The Art of Stress-Free Productivity*, transformed the world of planning with his revolutionary GTD method. His approach emphasizes capturing every task and idea into a trusted system, liberating mental space for creativity and strategic insight. By breaking larger projects into their very next actionable steps—a principle known as the "Next Action" method—Allen demonstrated that even the most daunting challenges could be managed with clarity and purpose.

His method mirrors the CCOPS framework by encouraging the clear capture of tasks, systematic clarification of goals, and meticulous organization into distinct categories. For instance, when preparing for an important project presentation, Allen would record every detail, sort them into relevant groups such as research, calls, or writing, and then prioritize crucial steps to maintain focus. This disciplined strategy not only reduced overwhelm and stress but also ignited creative problem-solving, turning chaotic ideas into a roadmap for success.

Allen's journey illustrates that effective planning is not merely about checking boxes—it's about crafting a structure that nurtures progress and fuels inspiration. His story invites you to embrace a method where every captured thought and organized task becomes a stepping stone toward achieving your dreams, proving that with the right tools, you too can transform ambition into tangible, everyday victories.

My Story

Like David Allen, I too had to confront my fears and redefine my approach to overcome daunting obstacles. Embracing his transformative strategy, I channeled setbacks into catalysts, igniting my journey toward a breakthrough as I Used the CCOPS Framework to Transform My Psychiatry Resident In Training Examination (PRITE) Performance

In my first year of residency (2021), I ranked in the 10th percentile on the Psychiatry Resident In Training Examination (PRITE)—a humbling start that fueled my determination to change. I embraced the CCOPS framework, and redefined how I approached every study session and task.

Starting with Capture, I set recurring calendar reminders for crucial tasks and transferred key items onto sticky notes. Every teaching moment and learning resource found its place in a single, ever-growing Word document—eventually spanning 470 pages. Difficult concepts, like personality types, were scheduled to reoccur monthly, ensuring they remained fresh in my mind. I even jotted down my ambitious target on paper: to skyrocket my performance from a low percentile to an eventual goal of 98th on my board exam.

Next, I moved to Clarify. Every day, I dedicated two pages of my notebook to a blend of gratitude, reflections, Bible insights, and lessons from books and podcasts. This ritual transformed vague aspirations into crystal-clear objectives. Instead of merely noting "improve my score," I detailed actionable steps—completing the Board Vitals Question Bank, tackling at least three past PRITE questions between exams, and even recording explanations for on-the-go review. Each task was given purpose, reinforcing my commitment not just to pass, but to excel as a psychiatrist for the benefit of my future patients.

Organizing became my sanctuary from mental clutter. I color-coded sticky notes and arranged tasks into well-defined categories. For instance, I broke down the daunting 1400 questions from the Board Vital Question Bank into a manageable goal of four questions per day. Every piece of information had its designated spot, creating a clear roadmap that streamlined my study sessions and prioritized what needed immediate attention.

Prioritizing was the next vital step. I assessed every task for its urgency and impact—practicing past exam questions emerged as the top priority, followed by reviewing my extensive notes, and then textbook reading. Inspired by Stephen Covey's four-quadrant system, I tackled high-impact tasks first. This disciplined focus propelled my PRITE performance from 10th percentile in my first year to an astounding 84th in my second, 92nd in my third, and 95th in my fourth year.

Finally, I learned to Simplify. Complex tasks were broken down into small, actionable steps that I could tackle daily. Instead of facing a mountain of 1400 questions at once, I saw them as a series of bite-sized, manageable actions—each one moving me closer to my goal without overwhelming me.

The CCOPS framework didn't just boost my exam scores—it transformed my approach to learning and personal growth. Each step of the process instilled a sense of order and clarity, turning chaos into a purposeful journey toward success.

Adapt and Advance

Effective planning doesn't eliminate challenges, but it equips you to overcome them. I discovered this firsthand as I faced critical moments that demanded the CCOPS framework. When preparing for the PRITE exam during residency, I captured every significant insight in a Word document. This meticulous record-keeping propelled me from the 10th percentile to the 92nd percentile over three years, proving that capturing every thought can be the first step toward transformative success.

When I migrated to the U.S. in 2014, leaving behind a secure position in Nigeria to pursue a new life, I turned to my notebooks filled with advice from mentors who had navigated similar transitions. These notes clarified my steps during a tumultuous time, ensuring a smoother journey by transforming uncertainty into actionable insight. During periods of overwhelming responsibility, such as balancing a PhD program with personal obligations, I relied on sticky notes and journals to organize my thoughts, keeping me grounded and focused on what truly mattered.

I also learned to prioritize by blocking weekly time for my personal values—serving God and my community—which kept me aligned with my mission despite the chaos. Simplifying complex projects into smaller, daily actions became a cornerstone of my strategy. In my PhD program, I divided my dissertation into manageable sections and completed them one at a time, a process that not only reduced my overwhelm but also provided clear, consistent progress.

Lessons from Scripture have been a guiding light through these challenges. Luke 14:28 reminds us that careful planning is essential for success; just as a builder calculates the cost before starting a tower, we must thoughtfully assess our resources, challenges, and steps toward our goals. This verse underscores the importance of preparation, realism, and focus—principles that have helped me turn daunting obstacles into achievable milestones.

Reflective quotes further solidified my commitment. Antoine de Saint-Exupéry's reminder that "A goal without a plan is just a wish" resonated deeply, urging me to transform dreams into tangible outcomes through disciplined planning.

The powerful imagery in Luke 14:28—"For which one of you, when he wants to build a watchtower [for his guards], does not first sit down and calculate the cost, to see if he has enough to finish it?"—calls us to approach our ambitions with realistic expectations and thoughtful intention. Just as a builder must plan meticulously, using the CCOPS framework has taught me to face challenges head-on, adapt to each situation, and advance steadily toward my dreams. Embracing these principles has transformed obstacles into stepping stones, empowering me to overcome personal challenges with resilience and clarity

Very Important Next Step

Devote just 15 minutes each day to immerse yourself in the CCOPS framework. In those brief moments, capture your thoughts, clarify your deepest goals, and organize your tasks into a clear plan—prioritizing actions and simplifying them into manageable steps. Every day, let this practice break down overwhelming challenges into small, achievable victories, reducing stress while fueling momentum. Set a timer, list your tasks, and uncover the "why" behind each one, categorizing them by work, family, or personal growth. Use sticky notes, a planner, or digital tools to keep your progress visible and your ideas aligned. With each intentional session, you're not only structuring your day but also building a definitive roadmap to transform your dreams into reality.

Worksheet or Exercise for Growth: Daily Planning Worksheet Using CCOPS

1. Capture: Write down all tasks, ideas, and goals for the day.

2. Clarify: Identify the purpose and desired outcome for each task.

3. Organize: Categorize tasks into meaningful groups.

4. Prioritize: Assign tasks to the four quadrants of importance/ urgency.

5. Simplify: Break large tasks into smaller, actionable steps.

Planning isn't about rigidity; it's about creating a roadmap for success while allowing flexibility. By practicing CCOPS daily, you'll build momentum and achieve your goals with clarity and peace of mind.

Now that you've learned to use CCOPS to plan effectively, the next chapter will focus on turning obstacles into stepping stones for greatness: The Obstacle in Your Plan Is the Road to Greatness.

CHAPTER 14

Plan B: The Obstacle in Your Plan Is the Road to Greatness

During a challenging time, a determined caterpillar refused to give up, knowing that every struggle was simply part of its transformation. One day, a butterfly flew by and asked, "Why are you crawling so slowly?"

The caterpillar replied, "I'm building strength for my wings."

The butterfly chuckled, dismissing it as nothing more than a worm with dreams. Yet the caterpillar persevered through storms, bird attacks, and even bad leaf buffets. In time, it emerged as a beautiful butterfly, soaring high, and returned to prove that difficulties aren't roadblocks—they're launchpads. Now, who's just a worm with dreams?

Like the caterpillar, we sometimes think we're stuck when in the actual sense, God is preparing us something greater. In this chapter, we will learn how to navigate obstacles and setbacks by embracing flexibility. Life rarely goes exactly as planned, but by creating backup plans (Plan B, C, or even D) and maintaining resilience, you can turn challenges into opportunities and move closer to your goals.

Embracing setbacks teaches us that obstacles can reveal inner strength and open unexpected pathways to growth. This insight is echoed in Marcus Aurelius' words, reminding us that challenges themselves can propel us forward.

> ."The impediment to action advances action.
> What stands in the way becomes the way."
> – Marcus Aurelius

How This Worked for Successful People: John D. Rockefeller

John D. Rockefeller, the wealthiest man in modern history, built his fortune by turning obstacles into opportunities. During the Panic of 1857, instead of succumbing to fear, he saw the downturn as a chance to study market trends and refine his business strategy. When railroad strikes disrupted oil transportation, he took control by building pipelines, reducing dependency on railroads, and creating long-term stability.

By breaking his grand vision into smaller, manageable steps— acquiring refineries, improving efficiency, and negotiating favorable rates—Rockefeller transformed every setback into a stepping stone toward success. When unstable kerosene markets threatened his progress, he leveraged creativity by diversifying into profitable byproducts like paraffin wax and lubricants, proving that adaptability is the key to thriving in adversity.

My Story

I found inspiration in Rockefeller's resilience as I faced my own hurdles. F ailing Chemistry in high school in 1994 was a major obstacle on my journey to becoming a medical doctor. Instead of surrendering, I viewed that failure as a chance to try again— re-enrolling, working harder, and trusting God to guide me. This renewed determination helped me pass the subject a year later, and eventually paved my way to medical school. Later, when a delay in residency admission occurred after my NYSC in 2006, I focused on what I could control by working as a medical officer and holding fast to God's promise in Hebrews 10:37 that "For yet in a very little while, He who is coming will come, and will not delay." My perseverance paid off as I was finally admitted into residency by 2007.

My transition from Nigeria to the U.S. in 2014 required immense faith and detailed planning. I broke this daunting journey into steps: securing a PhD admission for a student visa, applying for permanent residency, completing USMLE exams, undertaking a postdoctoral fellowship, and finally starting psychiatry residency. Over 11 years, I achieved my goal one step at a time by staying resilient and trusting God. During financial challenges, I practiced stoic calm, remaining composed and focused on my studies, work, and family, knowing that difficulties were temporary. After scoring in the 10th percentile on my first PRITE exam, I refused to accept defeat and innovated new study methods that propelled my score to the 84th percentile in PGY2, 92nd in PGY3, and 95th in PGY4.

Both Rockefeller's journey and my own demonstrate that resilience, creativity, and the willingness to break down challenges can transform obstacles into opportunities. By focusing on what we can control, embracing setbacks as learning moments, and persevering with faith, we too can overcome adversity and build the foundation for lasting success.

Adapt and Advance

Life's challenges may seem insurmountable, yet lessons from Scripture remind us that every setback has a purpose. Romans 8:28 reminds us that God uses every circumstance for our good. Even setbacks serve a greater purpose, shaping us for His glory and our ultimate success. Isaiah 43:2 reassures us of God's presence during trials. Waters and fire symbolize overwhelming challenges, but God promises to walk with us, ensuring we are not defeated. These verses teach us to trust God's sovereignty, knowing He turns obstacles into stepping stones for growth. For anyone feeling overwhelmed by life's uncertainties, these promises offer hope and a reminder that even our darkest moments are part of a divine plan.

A reflective quote from Marcus Aurelius, "The impediment to action advances action. What stands in the way becomes the way," echoes this truth by revealing that obstacles are opportunities in disguise. This Stoic principle reminds us that when we embrace challenges, we open pathways to growth and success. Whether you're facing career setbacks, personal losses, or unexpected changes, this insight encourages you to view each hindrance as a catalyst for progress and self-improvement.

Further deepening this perspective, the amplified message of Romans 8:28 (AMP) states, "And we know [with great confidence] that God [who is deeply concerned about us] causes all things to work together [as a plan] for good for those who love God, to those who are called according to His plan and purpose." This verse reassures us that no hardship is wasted, as every experience contributes to a divine, greater purpose. It reminds believers that challenges and setbacks ultimately serve our growth, molding us into resilient individuals. Trusting this promise fosters hope, enabling us to find meaning in trials and embrace life's journey with renewed determination.

Similarly, Isaiah 43:2 (AMP) proclaims, "When you pass through the waters, I will be with you; And through the rivers, they will not overwhelm you. When you walk through fire, you will not be scorched, nor will the flame burn you." This verse provides profound comfort during life's most turbulent moments, assuring us that even overwhelming challenges will not overpower us. It reminds us of God's constant presence and protection, offering hope and courage when navigating adversity. Trust in His promise enables us to face difficulties with resilience and unwavering faith, inspiring us to adapt, advance, and ultimately transform every obstacle into an opportunity for growth

Very Important Next Step

Each day, take 5–10 minutes to focus on one obstacle you're facing. Break it down into manageable steps and develop an alternative plan (Plan B) to move forward. This exercise transforms feelings of being stuck into proactive steps toward solutions. When you reduce challenges into smaller tasks, you ease overwhelm and gain clarity. By aligning your plans with God's guidance—as echoed in the wisdom of Romans 8:28 and Isaiah 43:2—setbacks evolve into opportunities for growth, much like the turning points in my own journey.

Reflect for a few minutes on the obstacles before you, jot them down, and pinpoint one small step you can take today. Use a journal or a simple to-do list to record your next actions, and revisit these plans daily, adjusting as needed to maintain progress. Every small action counts toward overcoming bigger hurdles. Embrace this approach by reframing one current obstacle as an opportunity, developing at least one alternative plan, and taking that small, consistent step each day toward your goal.

Worksheet or Exercise for Growth

Overcoming Obstacles Worksheet.

1. Identify a goal that has encountered obstacles.

2. List the challenges preventing progress.

3. Create a Plan B or backup strategy.

4. Break your Plan B into small, actionable steps.

5. Reflect on a Bible verse or quote that motivates you.

Adaptability and resilience are key to turning setbacks into success. By focusing on what you can control and trusting God's plan, you'll find the strength to advance, no matter the challenges.

Obstacles are not the end of the road but opportunities for redirection and growth. By creating backup plans and trusting God's guidance, we can turn challenges into stepping stones. In the next chapter, we'll focus on the power of wisdom and how one book can open doors to advancement.

SECTION 4
LIFELONG LEARNING

This section describes the critical role of learning in personal and professional advancement and consists of three chapters. Each chapter explores the transformative power of learning—both formal and informal—and provides actionable steps to help you align your education and growth with your life's purpose. The chapters in this section will guide you on how to utilize reading, conventional schooling, and continuous self-education to open doors to success, wisdom, and personal development.

In chapter 15 entitled "One Book. One Wisdom. One Open Door of Advancement," we will explore how reading books—especially books that align with your personal and professional growth goals—can serve as a key to unlocking doors of opportunity and advancement. It emphasizes the power of acquiring knowledge and wisdom that can be applied directly to your life's challenges and aspirations. Like Moses, whose wisdom from the Egyptians enabled him to lead with power, you too can be equipped to tackle obstacles and make informed decisions that shape your future. Regular reading and self-development are not just hobbies, but are powerful tools for personal transformation. This chapter will also reveal the importance of setting aside time each day for reading, whether through books or audiobooks, and integrating what you learn into your daily routine.

You'll discover how consistency in learning can transform your life and career, helping you adapt and advance. As you develop a mindset that embraces learning as a lifelong commitment, you'll find yourself in a continuous cycle of growth. The chapter also shares stories from both the Bible and real life to illustrate how the wisdom gained from reading can help you overcome difficulties, improve your leadership abilities, and enhance your resilience. By dedicating time to read daily, you open the door to new perspectives, insights, and strategies that prepare you for the challenges ahead.

In chapter 16 entitled "Conventional Schooling Still Works," we will explore the significant role conventional schooling plays in shaping our personal and professional lives. Despite the rise of alternative education methods and informal learning, formal education continues to provide the foundational knowledge and skills needed to excel in many areas of life. Conventional schooling nurtures critical thinking, discipline, and problem-solving skills while offering opportunities for social interaction and career advancement. You'll learn how pursuing higher education—whether through formal degrees, certifications, or specialized training—can expand your career opportunities and lead to personal growth.

Additionally, the chapter emphasizes that the educational journey often involves overcoming obstacles and setbacks. It shares personal stories, such as Ben Carson's triumph over adversity through education, and how my own experiences reflect the transformative power of formal schooling. The challenges we face during our educational journey often shape our character and resilience. By evaluating the importance of formal education in your life and setting clear academic goals, you can align your learning with your purpose. This chapter encourages you to embrace both the rewards and challenges of conventional schooling, knowing that your efforts today will contribute to your success in the future.

In chapter 17 entitled "Informal Learning Is Equally Important,", it shows that while conventional education provides essential knowledge, this chapter highlights how informal learning complements and enhances the education you receive through formal channels. Informal learning includes reading personal development books, listening to podcasts, engaging with educational content on YouTube, or participating in community discussions. This type of learning can often fill the gaps left by formal education, offering practical insights, personal growth strategies, and solutions to real-world problems. The chapter demonstrates how informal learning allows you to tailor your education to your unique goals, whether in leadership, career development, or spiritual growth.

Tony Robbins' story is a prime example of how informal learning can propel an individual to success. By committing to learning through books and seminars, Robbins was able to shape his career and achieve extraordinary accomplishments. Similarly, I share how my journey in informal learning through books and audio resources has helped me grow spiritually, personally, and professionally.

This chapter will equip you with practical strategies to incorporate informal learning into your daily life, using resources such as audiobooks, podcasts, and videos. You'll learn how to create a sustainable learning habit that nurtures your mind, expands your knowledge base, and helps you overcome challenges with confidence and resilience.

CHAPTER 15

One Book. One Wisdom. One Open Door of Advancement

W hy did the book go to school? Because it wanted to graduate into greatness!

In today's fast-paced world, knowledge is power. But not just any knowledge—knowledge acquired from focused, intentional, and continuous learning. Acquiring knowledge by reading books that align with your values and goals can open doors for you, leading to advancement in ways you never imagined. In this chapter, you will discover the transformative power of reading and self-development. You'll also learn how engaging with books that align with your values and goals can lead to new opportunities, wisdom, and personal advancement.

Embracing continuous learning transforms challenges into opportunities, fueling both growth and discovery. As Mark Twain reminds us, those who dismiss reading forfeit the key to unlocking hidden potential and success.

> "A person who won't read has no advantage over one who can't read."
>
> – Mark Twain

How This Worked for Successful People: Moses

Moses' leadership and influence were deeply rooted in the knowledge he acquired during his time in Egypt. Acts 7:22 highlights that he was educated in the wisdom of the Egyptians, preparing him to lead with power in both speech and action. Immersed in Egyptian wisdom, Moses harnessed this education to confront Pharaoh boldly, and to lead the Israelites through the wilderness.

His profound understanding of culture, strategy, and leadership allowed him to articulate a clear vision, inspire hope, and implement practical solutions in times of crisis. Rather than seeing obstacles as barriers, Moses turned them into stepping stones, using his knowledge to push towards freedom and prosperity for his people.

In the same vein, by embracing continuous learning, you too can gain the wisdom to positively influence your family, career, and community. Leadership begins at the point of knowledge acquisition, and each step taken strengthens your resolve, and stirs transformation within you and those around you. Moses' preparation is a timeless reminder that knowledge is foundational to success, and by intentionally seeking wisdom, we position ourselves to make a lasting impact. Just as Moses used his knowledge to lead and influence, you too can leverage the wisdom you gain to inspire and lead in your own life.

My Story

In 2001, after encountering God through Dr. David Oyedepo, I started reading approximately 52 books annually. This habit profoundly changed my life. Through books, I discovered my purpose, and learned strategies to navigate life's challenges, including the devastating loss of my parents at a young age. Books became my lifeline during dark seasons, illuminating my paths forward and teaching me resilience. Reading helped me adapt and advance through every phase of life.

Adapt and Advance

The lessons I've learned from reading have consistently equipped me to tackle new obstacles with faith and clarity. Through consistent learning, I've embraced Harry Truman's words that: "Not all readers become leaders, but all leaders must be readers." This truth resonates deeply, much like the timeless message in Acts 7:22, which tells us, "So Moses was educated in all the wisdom of the Egyptians, and he was [powerful] in his words and deeds." Moses' education empowered him to lead with purpose and confidence, turning his knowledge into action during the most critical moments of his life. His example reminds us that success begins with the pursuit of wisdom.

I also find inspiration in the words of Vera Nazarian: "Whenever you read a good book, somewhere in the world a door opens to allow in more light." Books offer clarity and solutions, helping us adapt and grow, even when life feels overwhelming. Margaret Fuller's assertion, "Today a reader, tomorrow a leader," further reinforces that every book we read plants the seeds for future advancement.

To harness this transformative power, I have developed practical strategies to help me read more: I set clear goals that align with my personal and professional aspirations and dedicate 15–30 minutes daily to reading or listening to audiobooks. I make the most of break times or commutes to absorb new ideas, leveraging technology like Audible, Kindle, or Blinkist for quick access to valuable insights.

I have cultivated a habit by starting small—just a few pages each day—gradually integrating reading into my daily routine, whether with morning coffee or as I wind down at night. Joining learning communities and book clubs has kept me motivated, while focusing on quality content ensures that my reading aligns with my growth goals.

I actively take notes and immediately apply the lessons I learn, reinforcing my understanding by using both audible and hard-copy versions. By delegating non-essential tasks, I free up more time for learning, tracking my progress in a journal, and celebrating every milestone. Each of these steps empowers me to transform obstacles into opportunities, continuously advancing my journey with the wisdom that reading provides.

Very Important Next Step

Every day, I commit 15–30 minutes to reading or listening to a motivational or spiritual book—choosing those that align with my personal and professional growth goals. This simple yet powerful habit has enriched my mind and equipped me with wisdom to navigate life's challenges. Just as Moses was educated in the wisdom of Egypt to lead with power, reading has provided me with the perspective needed to overcome setbacks, keeping me focused, adaptable, and ready to advance.

When I want to read, I choose a book that resonates with my goals, set aside dedicated time, and either read or listen intently, all while keeping a journal to capture key insights. One lesson from each book is applied immediately, ensuring steady progress in my life.

For instance, reading "The Purpose Driven Life" transformed my perspective, igniting a renewed sense of purpose that guides me daily. Its profound insights have helped me view every challenge as an opportunity for growth and reflection. Whenever difficulties arise, I recall its messages about faith, perseverance, and clarity of vision, drawing strength from my purpose every single day. This trusted companion has illuminated my path toward fulfillment and inspired me to push through obstacles with determination.

I encourage you to select one motivational or spiritual book this month, commit to at least 15 minutes of daily reading or listening, and apply one lesson immediately. This small, consistent action could be the very next step towards transforming your life.

Worksheet or Exercise for Growth: Your Personal Reading Plan

1. Identify a Book: Choose a motivational or spiritual book that aligns with your current goals.

2. Set a Schedule: Plan 15–30 minutes daily for reading or listening.

3. Take Notes: Write down key takeaways and action steps.

4. Apply Knowledge: Implement one insight from the book into your life this week.

5. Track Progress: Use a journal to monitor your learning journey.

Consistent reading is a gateway to wisdom and transformation. By investing in your personal growth through books, you equip yourself with tools to adapt, advance, and thrive through life's challenges.

Reading opens doors to wisdom, growth, and new opportunities. By prioritizing learning, you can transform your life and leadership. In the next chapter, we'll explore how conventional schooling continues to play a vital role in personal and professional advancement.

CHAPTER 16

Conventional Schooling Still Works

Why did the math book look sad? Because it knew that academic success starts with solving numerous problems! Academic success begins with solving challenges, and like the math book's sorrowful smile, every struggle conceals a unique opportunity. In this chapter, discover how relentless determination transforms setbacks into milestones of growth. From Ben Carson's inspiring journey to my own personal battles, learn how education forges resilience, fueling dreams into reality.

In this chapter, you will learn about the importance of conventional schooling. You'll discover how formal education can lay a foundation for personal and professional growth, equip you with essential life skills, and open doors to opportunities. If feasible, aim to pursue the level of education that aligns with your life's purpose, regardless of challenges.

Immersing yourself in formal education builds a robust foundation to navigate life's multifaceted challenges. These experiences affirm that learning transcends mere preparation—embodying life itself, as John Dewey so profoundly states.

"Education is not preparation for life; education is life itself."

—John Dewey

How This Worked for Successful People: Ben Carson

Ben Carson's life stands as a powerful testament to the transformative power of education. Born into poverty and burdened by early academic struggles, he defied the odds through the unwavering discipline his mother instilled in him. Despite her own limited education, she encouraged Carson to read two books every week, igniting a lifelong passion for learning that would redefine his destiny. This simple yet profound habit propelled him to excel academically, earning him a scholarship at Yale University, admission to the University of Michigan Medical School, and ultimately, the honor of becoming the youngest chief of pediatric neurosurgery at Johns Hopkins Hospital. Carson's journey illustrates that when determination and faith unite with conventional education, even the most challenging beginnings can lead to extraordinary success.

My Story

My journey in education has been one of continuous growth and transformation. I've navigated every level—from the early days of elementary, through middle and high school, to advanced studies reminiscent of a pre-med path. I earned my medical degree in Nigeria, followed by an internship and residency in Community Medicine. Determined to expand my horizons, I pursued a Master's in Public Health in Nigeria before moving to the U.S. to obtain a Ph.D. in Cancer Epidemiology. After completing postdoctoral training, I embarked on a Psychiatry residency, with graduation anticipated in 2025. Despite the many challenges at each stage, education has empowered me to adapt, advance, and embrace a lifelong journey of learning.

Adapt and Advance: Rising from Setbacks

The wisdom of Proverbs guides us in transforming trials into triumphs. Proverbs 1:5 reminds us, "A wise man will hear and increase in learning, and a man of understanding will acquire wise counsel." This verse teaches that true wisdom comes from continually listening and embracing new insights—even in our darkest moments. When challenges arise, seeking education and advice can help us turn setbacks into powerful tools for growth, enabling us to navigate life's obstacles with strength and grace.

Likewise, Proverbs 16:16 declares, "How much better it is to get wisdom than gold! And to get understanding is to be chosen above silver." This verse affirms that wisdom and understanding are treasures far more valuable than material wealth, illuminating our path and empowering us to conquer difficulties.

My own journey is a living testament to these truths. Failing Chemistry in high school was a setback that nearly derailed my dream of becoming a doctor. Trusting in God, I retook the exam the next year, worked harder, prayed, and succeeded—an experience that instilled in me resilience and faith.

Years later, after failing the USMLE Step One exam in 2018, I felt devastated. However, my children's heartfelt reminder of "Never give up" rekindled my determination. I re-took the exam in 2019 and passed, proving that setbacks are temporary when met with persistence and trust in God, as echoed in Proverbs 24:16: "For though the righteous fall seven times, they rise again."

Education, in all its forms, is a key part of our journey. It arms us with structured knowledge across diverse fields, fosters critical thinking and problem-solving, and nurtures interpersonal skills essential for both personal and professional growth. Beyond academic learning, education instills discipline, resilience, and a global perspective, encouraging active citizenship and social responsibility. Each lesson—whether derived from scripture, personal trials, or academic pursuits—serves as a stepping stone, gradually building the foundation for lasting success. Let these truths inspire you to persist, adapt, and advance, knowing that every challenge overcome is a victory on the path to a brighter future.

Very Important Next Step

Determine whether additional formal education aligns with your purpose, and if so, commit to it wholeheartedly, regardless of the obstacles you might face. Take one actionable step each day—whether that means researching schools, applying for a program, or beginning to study for entrance exams. By taking small steps daily, you steadily move closer to your goal.

Pursuing formal education, despite its challenges, can profoundly shape your personal and professional growth. Ben Carson's inspiring journey illustrates how education can transform a life of struggle into one filled with purpose and success. Embracing this path has not only endowed me with knowledge but also the resilience required to overcome obstacles.

To make progress, set aside five to ten minutes each day to assess your educational goals. Use that time to research programs, draft a study plan, or revisit materials relevant to your field. Break larger goals into smaller, manageable tasks to ensure you remain aligned with your purpose, and keep a journal of your progress and challenges to stay focused and motivated.

Worksheet or Exercise for Growth

1. Self-Assessment: List your educational achievements and the challenges you overcame.

2. Goal Setting: Identify one educational goal and outline steps to achieve it.

3. Daily Action: Commit to one small task daily to move closer to your goal (e.g., researching a program, reviewing a textbook).

Education equips you to adapt and thrive through life's challenges.

Seek God's guidance in every educational pursuit, trusting His plan for your life.

Conventional schooling remains a powerful tool for personal growth and resilience. As we transition into the next chapter, we'll explore how informal learning complements formal education, proving that all forms of learning are equally vital.

CHAPTER 17

Informal Learning Is Equally Important

A man walks into a library and asks the librarian, 'Do you have any books on self-improvement?' The librarian points to a large section and says, "Over there, but I have to warn you—they're all self-serve."

The words of this librarian shades light on the realities of informal education. While conventional education provides a strong foundation, informal learning offers the adaptability and practical insights needed for lifelong growth. In this chapter, we'll explore how self-education, through books, podcasts, and observation, can propel you beyond what's taught in the classroom

In this chapter, you will discover how informal learning complements formal education and, in some cases, surpasses it in value. We'll explore practical ways to embrace continuous self-education through reading, listening, and observing, and how these habits can propel you toward success in every area of life.

Every insight gathered beyond formal classrooms lays the foundation for personal transformation. As Charlie Tremendous Jones reminds us, our evolution is shaped by the connections we forge and the knowledge we gain.

"You will be the same person in five years as you are today except for the people you meet and the books you read."

—Charlie Tremendous Jones

How This Worked for Successful People: Tony Robbins.

Tony Robbins, the world-renowned life strategist, attributes much of his success to his commitment to informal learning. As a young man, Robbins set a goal to read one book per day, primarily on psychology and personal development. Although he didn't always achieve his daily target, over seven years, he read more than 700 books.

This relentless self-education helped him understand human behavior deeply, shaping his strategies for success. Robbins built his empire by sharing actionable insights through his books, seminars, and coaching programs, inspiring millions worldwide. Today, his net worth exceeds $600 million, proving that a dedication to lifelong learning can lead to extraordinary achievements.

My Story

In 2000, after joining Living Faith Church in Nigeria, I embarked on a transformative journey of informal learning by delving into books by Bishop David Oyedepo. The first book I read, *Towards Mental Exploits*, completely reshaped my perspective and inspired me to commit to reading one book a week. Although I haven't always been consistent, this practice has profoundly influenced my personal and professional growth over the years.

Initially, I absorbed knowledge through physical books, but as technology evolved, I transitioned to audiobooks on Audible, seamlessly integrating learning into my daily routine. Beyond personal development, I also dedicated myself to spiritual enrichment by listening to sermons from seven different pastors— one for each day of the week. This lifelong commitment to learning has not only supported my formal education but has also guided my journey in marriage, career, parenting, and spirituality, continually transforming my life.

Adapt and Advance

Over 24 years of consistent informal learning, I have witnessed remarkable growth in every area of my life. Books have not only strengthened my relationship with God by offering insights that help me align with His purpose, but they have also fortified my 17-year marriage and guided my wife and I as we raise our twin boys. Informal learning has provided me with practical tools to manage my marriage, parent my children, and navigate my career.

Books and sermons have been more than just sources of knowledge—they have empowered me to make better decisions and face life's challenges with unwavering confidence. Professionally, the wisdom I've acquired has allowed me to overcome obstacles, maintain focus, and reach significant milestones, complementing my formal education by fostering resilience and fueling continuous self-improvement.

Increased self-awareness has come from embracing learning that challenges me to reflect on my strengths and weaknesses. For instance, reading *The 7 Habits of Highly Effective People* opened my eyes to my personal patterns and helped me set clearer intentions, teaching me how to adjust my behavior and align my decisions with my vision for the future.

Enhanced problem-solving skills, nurtured by works like *Thinking, Fast and Slow*, have given me practical strategies to break down complex issues into manageable parts, transforming challenges into opportunities for creative solutions both at work and in personal life. Continuous learning, whether through motivational podcasts during my commute or reflective reading sessions, has kept me inspired and goal-oriented, turning mundane routines into moments of purposeful progress even when obstacles arise.

Stronger relationships are built on the foundation of emotional intelligence, a quality enhanced by engaging with authors like Brené Brown. Their insights have deepened my empathy and communication skills, helping me forge genuine connections with friends, family, and colleagues.

As Ecclesiastes 7:12 (AMP) reminds us, "For wisdom is a protection even as money is a protection, but the advantage of knowledge is that wisdom shields and preserves the lives of its possessors." I have experienced this truth firsthand as insights from books have provided me with the tools to navigate personal crises and safeguard my well-being.

Recognizing that all true wisdom comes from above, Daniel 1:17 (AMP) declares, "God gave them knowledge and skill in all learning and wisdom." This verse inspires me to seek God's guidance in every study, knowing that genuine understanding is a divine gift enriching every aspect of my life. Moreover, studying not only enhances our worldly knowledge but also strengthens our spirituality. As 2 Timothy 2:15 (AMP) urges, "Study and do your best to present yourself to God approved." By dedicating time to both scripture and spiritual literature, I have deepened my faith and discovered a steady source of inner peace and purpose.

The Bible further emphasizes the importance of knowledge with Hosea 4:6 (AMP): "My people are destroyed for lack of knowledge [of My law, where I reveal My will]." This powerful reminder teaches that ignorance can lead to destruction, urging us to seek knowledge daily. Through informal learning, I have come to understand that every book I read, every podcast I listen to, transforms trials into triumphs. Each lesson is a stepping stone, paving the way for enduring personal growth. Embracing education not only shields us in times of crisis but also illuminates our path, ensuring that we continually evolve, overcome, and advance in every area of our lives.

Very Important Next Step

Choose a personal development book, podcast, or video series this month and commit to at least 15 minutes of focused learning daily. Even these small, consistent blocks of time can compound into powerful growth over time. Informal learning not only enhances problem-solving skills but also strengthens relationships and increases self-awareness. It builds resilience, provides actionable insights, and aligns you with the wisdom needed to navigate life's challenges and triumphs. Start by selecting a resource in an area you wish to grow, then dedicate 10–15 minutes each day—during your commute, break times, or before bed—to immerse yourself in its lessons. Take notes and reflect on how these insights can transform your life.

Worksheet or Exercise for Growth

1. Reflection: List three areas of your life where you want to grow.

2. Action Plan: Identify one book, podcast, or video series to study in each area over the next month.

3. Daily Habit: Commit to 15 minutes of focused learning daily.

Informal learning is a lifelong journey.

Seek God's wisdom as the ultimate source of knowledge.

Informal learning provides the tools to continuously adapt and thrive. As we transition into the next chapter, let's explore how to craft a personal mission statement to align your learning with your life's purpose.

SECTION 5
ALLIANCE

This section describes the transformative power of relationships and how they help us thrive under stress and beyond mere survival. It consists of two chapters: Chapter 18, *How Supportive Relationships Can Help You Thrive Under Stress*, and Chapter 19, *Beyond Survival: Leveraging the Power of Relationships to Give Back and Transform Lives*. These chapters explore the invaluable role that supportive relationships play in building resilience and enabling personal growth, as well as how leveraging these relationships can amplify our impact and extend our reach.

In Chapter 18, entitled *How Supportive Relationships Can Help You Thrive Under Stress*, we examine the profound effects of meaningful connections on mental and emotional well-being. Stress is an inevitable part of life, but having supportive relationships can make all the difference. From friendships and mentorships to family bonds, the power of empathy and trust forms the foundation of resilience.

You'll learn how emotional regulation, attachment figures, and social connection help buffer stress and navigate adversity. Through stories of renowned figures like Oprah Winfrey and Michelle Obama, as well as personal testimonies, this chapter highlights how these relationships act as life preservers, helping us weather life's most challenging storms. You'll also discover actionable strategies for nurturing gratitude in relationships and how these actions further strengthen your emotional fortitude.

In Chapter 19, entitled *Beyond Survival: Leveraging the Power of Relationships to Give Back and Transform Lives*, we move beyond simply surviving to thriving through relationships. The emphasis here is on how relationships can serve as a vehicle for giving back and creating a lasting legacy. Whether it's building trust, fostering personal connections, or engaging in meaningful collaborations, relationships are essential for turning personal success into collective empowerment.

Using examples from people like Tony Robbins, Malala Yousafzai, and Dwayne "The Rock" Johnson, the chapter demonstrates how giving and collaborating with others can exponentially increase impact. In addition to personal stories, you will explore how consistency, emotional resonance, and reciprocity can deepen bonds and create a network of mutual support. Through practical exercises and reflective activities, you'll learn how to engage with your community and leverage these connections to not only elevate your own life but to lift others as well.

In both chapters, the importance of empathy and mutual support is emphasized, showing how these qualities build trust, create lasting connections, and provide the strength necessary to overcome life's hurdles. These relationships do not just sustain us—they propel us forward, turning adversity into opportunities for growth. Whether you are facing challenges or looking to give back to those around you, these chapters provide a roadmap for transforming your relationships into sources of empowerment and resilience.

CHAPTER 18

How Supportive Relationships Can Help You Thrive Under Stress

W hy did the stressed-out coffee bean go to therapy? Because it couldn't espresso itself! But then it found a supportive sugar cube who said, "Don't worry, bean buddy, I'm here to sweeten your life!" Together, they brewed a strong friendship and realized: with the right support, any bitter situation can turn into something sweet.

Imagine you're facing the toughest period of your life: job loss, health issues, or personal grief. Now imagine facing it alone—no one to lean on, no one to share the burden. The weight would feel unbearable. But, what if you had someone beside you, offering a listening ear or a helping hand?

In this chapter, you'll discover how supportive relationships act as a foundation for resilience. Drawing from research, personal testimonies, and biblical wisdom, we'll uncover the power of friendships, mentorships, and empathy in buffering stress and overcoming adversity. Whether it's childhood trauma, personal setbacks, or life's everyday challenges, you'll learn how meaningful connections can transform your journey.

"Friendship is the only cement that will
ever hold the world together."
– Woodrow Wilson

How This Worked for Successful People: The Power of Supportive Relationships.

Oprah Winfrey credits her grandmother for providing love and stability during a difficult childhood. Despite the toxic stress of poverty and abuse, her grandmother's care created a foundation of resilience, allowing her to rise above her circumstances and build a life of incredible impact.

Michelle Obama's deep bond with her parents, especially her father, instilled in her emotional stability and resilience. Their constant encouragement helped her navigate challenges with grace and determination, shaping the confident and inspirational leader she would become.

J.K. Rowling endured personal struggles and relentless rejections before the success of *Harry Potter*, but through it all, she leaned on friends for encouragement. Their support sustained her, keeping her persistent even when the odds seemed impossible.

Trevor Noah's mother showed unwavering empathy despite the hardships they faced under apartheid. Her love and resilience restored his trust and shaped his path to success.

My Story

Just like Oprah and her grandmother, my father, Solomon Adetunji Babatunde, became my rock after my mother passed away. For five years, he filled the void with unwavering support, ensuring I lacked nothing. Even his new wife welcomed me with kindness, making me feel loved and secure. Those years with my father taught me the irreplaceable power of showing up for the people we love, proving that support creates a safe space for growth, helping us face life's toughest moments with strength.

Similar to Michelle Obama's story, after losing both of my parents, three individuals stepped into my life as attachment figures: Lydia, Maria, and Israel. Lydia, though not wealthy, supported me as if I were her own. Maria opened her home to me during difficult times, ensuring I always had a place to belong. Israel, a humble farmer, provided food from his farm, reminding me that even in loss, love and kindness endure. Their unwavering support kept me grounded and hopeful, reinforcing that attachment figures, even outside of traditional family roles, provide stability and emotional grounding that help us weather life's storms.

Similar to J.K. Rowling's story, after my father passed away, his friend Enoch also stepped in at many critical moments to guide me in my journey. Knowing my father had dreamed of me becoming a doctor, Enoch encouraged me to pursue medicine, supporting me through applications and residency. Whenever I doubted myself, he reminded me of my purpose, keeping me focused on the goal. His mentorship drove my success, and that showed me that social support strengthens and inspires us to pursue greater dreams.

In my life, my wife, Bukky, has been my anchor for 17 years, similar to how Trevor Noah's mother showed unwavering empathy. Despite my struggles in expressing emotions, she has embraced me fully, offering unshakable empathy and understanding. Even through years of delayed gratification during my studies and residency, she stood by me, her unwavering support never faltering. Bukky, your love means the world to me. You have taught me that empathy creates a space for trust and healing, making resilience possible even in the face of adversity

Adapt and Advance

Life's challenges can feel overwhelming, but the power of relationships, support, and faith enables us to rise above them. As Galatians 6:2 reminds us, "Carry each other's burdens, and in this way, you will fulfill the law of Christ." We were never meant to walk this journey alone. True strength is seen when we support one another. Whether through family, friends, or even kind strangers, sharing each other's struggles fosters mutual resilience and reflects the love that Christ calls us to embody.

Ecclesiastes 4:9-10 reinforces this truth: "Two are better than one because they have a good return for their labor: If either of them falls down, one can help the other up." There will be moments when we stumble—when the weight of loss, failure, or disappointment threatens to hold us down. In these times, the presence of a supportive friend, mentor, or loved one can make all the difference. It is in these moments of shared struggle that we find renewed strength, realizing that resilience is not about standing alone but about lifting one another up.

Proverbs 17:17 further deepens this understanding: "A friend loves at all times, and a brother is born for adversity." True friendships are not measured by convenience, but by the ability to withstand life's storms together. When hardships arise, real friends remain steadfast, offering not just words of comfort but also unwavering presence. These bonds become a refuge, a source of hope and encouragement when everything else feels uncertain. Very Important Next Step

Each day, take a moment to recognize and appreciate those who have supported you. Whether it was a kind word, a thoughtful action, or simply their presence during a difficult moment, acknowledging their role in your life strengthens both your resilience and your relationships. A simple act of gratitude—writing down their name, sending a message, making a call, or offering a prayer—can deepen your connection and reinforce the support network that carries you through life's challenges.

Gratitude is more than a feeling; it's a powerful force that fosters emotional well-being and reinforces a positive mindset. When we intentionally reflect on the kindness of others, we shift our focus from stress to appreciation, reminding ourselves that we are not alone. This daily habit nurtures resilience, making it easier to navigate adversity with a heart full of gratitude and hope.

At the end of each day, take just a few moments to write down the name of one person who supported you. It could be a family member who encouraged you, a friend who checked in, a mentor who offered wisdom, or even a stranger whose kindness brightened your day. Express your gratitude in a tangible way—send a message, make a quick call, or whisper a prayer for them. This simple yet intentional practice will not only strengthen your relationships but will also help you cultivate a mindset of appreciation, allowing you to thrive even in the face of life's difficulties.

Worksheet or Exercise for Growth

1. Reflection Exercise:

- Who are your top three supportive relationships?
- How do they contribute to your resilience?

2. Daily Action Plan:

- Reach out to one person daily with encouragement or gratitude.
- Dedicate time weekly to a supportive community or mentorship activity.

3. Empathy Practice:

- The next time someone shares their feelings, listen without offering solutions.

4. Journal Prompt:

- Reflect on a time when a relationship helped you overcome adversity. What made that connection impactful?

Supportive relationships are a gift, both to give and to receive. As you practice gratitude, nurture connections, and show empathy, you'll find that your resilience grows stronger, enabling you to face life's challenges with confidence and grace.

Supportive relationships are not just a buffer against stress but a cornerstone for resilience. As we embrace and nurture these connections, we build a life anchored in trust, empathy, and shared purpose. In the next chapter, we'll explore how giving back and building relationships rooted in generosity can transform lives and create a lasting legacy.

CHAPTER 19

Beyond Survival: Leveraging the Power of Relationships to Give Back and Transform Lives

Why did the ladder refuse to climb alone? Because it realized success isn't about solo steps—it's about leaning on relationships! So, it partnered with a tree for shade, a hammer for strength, and a rope for flexibility. Together, they built a bridge for others. Even a ladder knows that relationships transform lives!

Just like the ladder found strength in partnership, we, too, achieve more when we lean on supportive relationships. History is filled with examples of individuals who transformed their lives and careers through trust, collaboration, and meaningful connections.

Success isn't a solo journey—it thrives on trust, connection, and collaboration. Whether in personal life or professional growth, meaningful connections amplify success, foster resilience, and open doors to opportunities that would be impossible alone.

In this chapter, we explore how leveraging relationships can transform both your life and the lives of others. Through examples of trust, personalization, collaboration, and community engagement, we'll uncover how relationships are key to thriving.

You'll learn practical ways to build meaningful connections that inspire growth, foster loyalty, and amplify impact.

Strong relationships not only provide support, but also create opportunities for growth, success, and shared purpose. As Oprah Winfrey and Helen Keller remind us, the right connections elevate our potential and make even the impossible achievable.

> "Alone we can do so little; together we can do so much."
>
> – Helen Keller

How This Worked for Successful People: Leveraging the Power of Relationships to Give Back and Transform Lives

Harnessing the power of relationships goes beyond merely making connections—it is the key to lasting success and personal transformation. Throughout history, individuals who have built trust, personalized their interactions, and engaged with their communities have made more impact than they could have achieved alone.

Oprah Winfrey, for example, built immense trust with her audience by being authentic and vulnerable the way most people weren't willing to be. By sharing her personal struggles and triumphs, she created an enduring connection with millions. Personalization is another key to building strong relationships. J.K. Rowling's ability to connect with readers through themes of love, loss, and perseverance made her stories feel deeply personal and relatable.

Beyond trust and personalization, emotional resonance is what turns a connection into something deeply impactful. Tyler Perry's storytelling touches audiences because it addresses real-life struggles, faith, and forgiveness—universal themes that evoke deep emotion. Reciprocity plays a crucial role in building loyalty and lasting relationships. Tony Robbins created a devoted following by offering free seminars and empowerment tools, demonstrating generosity before asking for anything in return.

Consistency is another factor that strengthens relationships and establishes reliability. Serena Williams exemplifies this principle through her relentless dedication on and off the court. Her consistent presence in sports, philanthropy, and social media has made her a trusted and inspiring figure.

Beyond individual relationships, community engagement amplifies impact. Malala Yousafzai didn't just fight for her own right to education—she built a global movement by encouraging others to share their stories and join her advocacy.

Collaboration expands reach and unlocks new opportunities. Dwayne "The Rock" Johnson has leveraged partnerships with brands and influencers to extend his impact into multiple industries.

My Story

Like Oprah Winfrey, I have experienced this truth firsthand in my role as a volunteer for a younger group at church. Teaching with transparency and sharing my personal devotional notes allows me to connect deeply with those I mentor. I've seen how openness fosters engagement and trust, proving that authenticity is the foundation of meaningful relationships. Applying the principle of personalization, like J.K. Rowling, when the older group of boys I mentored graduated from high school, I continued to send them personalized daily devotionals. Years later, they still express appreciation for these messages, demonstrating how thoughtful, tailored interactions leave a lasting impact. Taking the time to understand and value others strengthens relationships in ways that generic gestures cannot.

My own journey during my PhD was filled with rejections in grant applications and publications, but those setbacks ultimately paved the way for a breakthrough—a $500,000 grant that far outweighed all the previous disappointments. Sharing this story of perseverance with others has inspired them to push forward despite obstacles. When we open up about our struggles and triumphs, we connect on a human level, encouraging and uplifting those around us.

In terms of reciprocity, I experienced a similar principle in 2009 when I began hosting free success seminars in Nigeria. These events became platforms for empowerment, reinforcing the importance of giving back. When we invest in others without expecting immediate returns, we build strong, loyal relationships that create long-term impact.

Since 2009, I have committed to consistency in mentoring and sharing motivational content. Over the years, this dedication has fostered trust and reliability among those I engage with, proving that showing up regularly is key to maintaining strong relationships.

I have been blessed by the power of supportive communities throughout my journey. From faith-based groups to professional networks, these communities have offered encouragement and growth opportunities that I could not have accessed alone. Being part of a supportive group fosters mutual growth and shared success.

Similar to Dwayne "The Rock" Johnson, throughout my academic journey, collaborating with mentors and peers has opened doors I couldn't have walked through alone. These partnerships have enriched my learning and broadened my influence, reaffirming that teamwork multiplies potential.

The transformative power of relationships cannot be overstated. Whether through trust, personalization, emotional resonance, reciprocity, consistency, community engagement, or collaboration, strong connections are the foundation of success. Investing in relationships not only helps us grow but also empowers us to uplift others, ensuring that our impact extends far beyond ourselves.

Adapt and Advance

Life is not meant to be navigated alone. The challenges we face, the burdens we carry, and the successes we celebrate are all more meaningful when shared with others. Proverbs 3:5-6 reminds us to "Trust in the Lord with all your heart and lean not on your own understanding; in all your ways submit to Him, and He will make your paths straight." Trusting in God mirrors the trust we build in relationships—both require surrender, vulnerability, and faith. Just as we rely on God to guide our steps, we must also learn to lean on the support of those around us. True strength is not in isolation but in the willingness to depend on others, knowing that the right relationships can help us overcome even the toughest challenges.

Galatians 6:2 urges us to "Carry each other's burdens, and in this way, you will fulfill the law of Christ." Life's hardships become lighter when we share them. Whether it's offering a listening ear, a word of encouragement, or a helping hand, supporting others deepens our connections and strengthens both the giver and the receiver.

In a world that often prioritizes independence, it is easy to forget the power of community. But every time we show up for someone, we reflect Christ's love and remind them they are not alone. Small acts of kindness, consistent check-ins, and moments of selfless giving create a foundation of trust that we can all lean on when the weight of life becomes too heavy to bear alone.

Ecclesiastes 4:9-10 further reinforces this truth: "Two are better than one because they have a good return for their labor. If either of them falls down, one can help the other up." There will be moments in life when we stumble—when setbacks shake our confidence, when failure feels overwhelming, or when the road ahead seems too uncertain. But in those moments, the presence of a supportive friend, mentor, or loved one can make all the difference.

Collaboration and mutual support don't just make life easier; they make success more fulfilling. When we surround ourselves with the right people—those who lift us up, challenge us to grow, and walk alongside us in both triumph and struggle—we create a network of resilience that carries us through even the most difficult seasons.

The key to strengthening these relationships is intentional action. Each day, take a small step to reach out to someone—a friend, a colleague, a family member—and offer encouragement or support. A simple text message, a phone call, or a heartfelt note can have a profound impact. Investing in relationships isn't about grand gestures; it's about consistency. The more we nurture our connections, the stronger they become, creating a cycle of support that lifts everyone involved. In doing so, we not only enrich our own lives but also contribute to a world where kindness, trust, and love are the foundation of lasting success.

Very Important Next Step

Relationships are the foundation of resilience and success. Every meaningful connection we build strengthens our ability to thrive, especially during difficult times. Just as we've seen throughout this chapter, relationships provide the emotional support, encouragement, and trust needed to push forward when challenges arise. A small act of connection each day can transform lives—both yours and those around you. By making the effort to reach out, encourage, or support someone, you create lasting bonds that nurture growth, deepen empathy, and amplify positive impact.

Start by setting aside just 5–10 minutes each day to connect with someone. It could be as simple as sending a text, making a quick call, or offering a thoughtful word of encouragement. A handwritten note, a kind gesture, or simply taking the time to ask how someone is doing can make a profound difference. Personalizing your communication—showing genuine interest and empathy—builds trust and strengthens relationships over time. These small daily actions accumulate, creating a network of support that sustains you and others through life's highs and lows.

Take a moment to reflect on the people who have shaped your journey. Who are the top three individuals who have impacted your life in a meaningful way? How can you show gratitude or give back to them? Consider setting a daily connection practice—identifying one person each day to encourage, assist, or connect with in a meaningful way. Think about collaboration as well. Is there a project or goal where working with others could amplify your success? Write down one initiative where partnering with the right people could accelerate progress.

Finally, begin crafting a personal mission statement that reflects the relationships you value and the impact you want to create. Meaningful connections don't just happen; they are built intentionally through consistent actions and genuine care. By prioritizing relationships, you not only enrich your own life but also become a source of strength, encouragement, and transformation for others

Relationships are a powerful force for transformation. Whether it's through trust, emotional resonance, or collaboration, investing in meaningful connections creates a ripple effect of positive change.

Transforming lives goes beyond survival; it's about leveraging relationships to give back, inspire growth, and create lasting change. By building trust, personalizing interactions, and fostering collaboration, you amplify your impact and deepen connections. In the next chapter, we'll explore how to Draft a Personal Mission Statement—a guiding principle that aligns your values, purpose, and goals. Let's move forward and discover how to create a vision for your life.

SECTION 6

MISSION STATEMENT

This section describes the journey of aligning your life with purpose, direction, and action, and consists of four chapters. In these chapters, you will be equipped with the tools needed to craft a life-driven by intention. Each chapter will guide you in taking concrete steps to write your personal mission statement, decide on your values, prioritize essential roles, and set both long- and short-term goals, all while fostering a deeper sense of spiritual connection and motivation. Through practical advice, powerful stories, and biblical wisdom, you will learn how to live with intention, structure, and faith.

In chapter 20, entitled "Draft a Personal Mission Statement," we begin by understanding the significance of having a clear sense of direction in life. Your personal mission statement serves as a compass, offering you focus and motivation even in times of difficulty. This chapter will help you create a personal mission statement that aligns with your faith and guides you through life's challenges. By breaking down the key components—focus, purpose, and function—you'll be empowered to define what truly matters to you. With a strong mission statement, you'll gain clarity and drive, enabling you to make decisions that align with your values and goals.

In chapter 21, entitled "Decide on Your Values," you will explore the vital role that values play in shaping who you are and guiding your decisions. Your values form the foundation of your character and determine how you navigate the world. This chapter will help you identify your core values and integrate them into your mission statement. By understanding what matters most to you, you can stay grounded and focused on your goals. With a clear understanding of your values, you'll be equipped to live a life of integrity and purpose, ensuring that your actions reflect what you hold most dear.

In chapter 22, entitled "Prioritize the Roles That Are Important to You," we dive deeper into how to manage the responsibilities that matter most. Whether it's your role as a parent, partner, professional, or spiritual leader, each role plays a crucial part in shaping your path. This chapter will help you identify and prioritize these roles to ensure that you live a balanced, intentional life. Through reflection and personal stories, you'll learn how focusing on your key roles will help you navigate challenges, honor your commitments, and stay aligned with your mission and values.

In chapter 23, entitled "The Power of 'I Am' Statements," you will uncover how affirmations can transform your mindset and empower you to overcome obstacles. The words you speak to yourself have the power to shape your reality. This chapter teaches you how to create daily affirmations that align with your mission, values, and roles. By speaking positive declarations over your life, you will build confidence, resilience, and clarity. These "I am" statements will serve as powerful reminders of your identity and purpose, helping you maintain focus and determination as you pursue your goals.

In chapter 24, entitled "Set Long-Term and Short-Term Goals," you will learn the importance of breaking your mission into actionable steps. With your mission, values, and roles clearly defined, you will now set both long-term and short-term goals to guide your journey. This chapter provides practical tools for setting goals using the SMART framework—ensuring that your goals are specific, measurable, achievable, relevant, and time-bound. By setting clear goals, you will create a roadmap that leads you toward your dreams, keeping you motivated and on track as you work toward your vision for the future.

CHAPTER 20

Draft a Personal Mission Statement

Why did the lost traveler stop wandering aimlessly? He finally wrote down his destination! Without direction, he kept circling back to the same struggles. But with a clear purpose, every step had meaning. Even life's detours became part of the journey. A mission statement is the map that guides transformation.

In this chapter, you will learn the importance of creating a personal mission statement and discover step-by-step guidance on how to write one. A mission statement serves as a compass, giving your life purpose and direction. It will empower you to stay focused, grounded, and inspired, no matter the challenges you face.

A well-crafted mission statement not only shapes your decisions but also influences those around you, creating a ripple effect of purpose. As Stephen R. Covey emphasizes, defining your mission is one of the most powerful steps you can take toward personal and leadership growth.

> "The single most important and far-reaching leadership activity that you will ever do is to develop a personal mission statement—and then to bring that sense of mission, of purpose, to your family."
>
> – Stephen R. Covey

How This Worked for Successful People: Stephen R. Covey on Personal Mission Statement

In *The 7 Habits of Highly Effective People*, Stephen R. Covey emphasized the power of a personal mission statement through Habit 2: "Begin with the End in Mind." Covey shared how individuals and organizations thrive when they define their core values and long-term goals. He gave the example of a man who reconnected with his family after writing a mission statement centered on love and service. Covey also detailed how mission statements guide decisions and align actions with purpose, helping people live intentionally rather than reactively—building character, clarity, and lasting effectiveness.

My Story

In 2000, I embarked on a journey of personal development, committing to reading one self-help book each week. Among the many books that shaped my thinking, *The 7 Habits of Highly Effective People* by Stephen Covey stood out the most. It resonated deeply, shifting my mindset and inspiring me to craft my first mission statement: *"Clothing men with knowledge to reach the top."* At the time, I didn't have everything figured out, but I trusted the process. I learned that clarity comes through action, and embracing this purpose transformed my life in ways I could have never imagined.

With this mission driving me, I sought opportunities to serve. I joined two teaching teams in my local church, eager to impart knowledge and help others grow. Every Monday, I taught the Holy Spirit class to new believers at the Believers' Foundation School, and on Sundays, I led teachings in the Home Cell Unit. In dedicating myself to this work, I unknowingly stepped into one of the greatest blessings of my life—it was through this mission-driven service that I met my wife. To this day, her presence enriches my life, reinforcing how purpose aligns us with the right people at the right time.

Beyond teaching, my commitment to sharing knowledge took on new forms. I launched a monthly seminar, creating a platform to empower others, and for five years, I published a four-page monthly journal, filled with insights and encouragement. Yet, my path was not without struggles. The loss of my parents brought financial hardship, and academic difficulties in medical school threatened to derail my progress.

But in those moments of uncertainty, my mission statement became my anchor. It reminded me of my purpose and kept me focused, driving me forward when circumstances could have easily made me quit. Through all the ups and downs, I learned that when you define your mission and commit to it, even in the face of challenges, life becomes an adventure filled with meaning, growth, and unshakable purpose.

Adapt and Advance

Life brings financial struggles, academic setbacks, and personal losses, but having a clear mission provides the strength to persevere. Rather than dwelling on difficulties, I chose to focus on my purpose, and let my mission statement serve as a guiding light. My mission evolved over time, but its core remained the same—offering clarity, motivation, and direction. Today, my mission statement reflects my journey, my faith, and my commitment to making a positive impact: *"To fulfill God's purpose as I succeed in life, moving from one level of success and value to a higher level of success and value per time, and to contribute positively to the success of others that God places in my path."* This statement is more than just words; it is a declaration of intent, a reminder of why I push forward despite the challenges.

John 20:21 (AMP) states, *"Then Jesus said to them again, 'Peace to you; as the Father has sent Me, I also send you [as My representatives].'"* Just as Jesus was sent with a purpose, we, too, are meant to live with intention. A personal mission statement gives our lives clarity and meaning, ensuring that every step we take aligns with our higher calling. When difficulties arise, it becomes our anchor, keeping us steady and reminding us why we started in the first place.

Writing down your mission is one of the most powerful ways to solidify it. Habakkuk 2:2 (AMP) reminds us of this: *"Then the Lord answered me and said, 'Write the vision And engrave it plainly on [clay] tablets So that the one who reads it will run.'"* Writing your mission statement makes it tangible, transforming an abstract idea into a concrete commitment. When clearly documented, it keeps you focused and motivated. More importantly, your mission must be anchored in God's divine plan. Jeremiah 29:11 (AMP) reassures us: *"For I know the plans and thoughts that I have for you,' says the Lord, 'plans for peace and well-being and not for disaster, to give you a future and a hope.'"* Even in uncertainty, we can trust that God's plans are for our good. When we align our personal mission with His purpose, we find peace, confidence, and direction. Instead of feeling lost, we step forward with faith, knowing that every challenge we face is shaping us for something greater.

Crafting a personal mission statement requires deep reflection. Ask yourself : What is your focus? Why are you here? What role will you play? For example, my focus is to fulfill God's purpose, my purpose is to grow in success and value, and my function is to positively impact others. Whether simple or detailed, your mission statement should resonate deeply with you, acting as a personal blueprint for how you want to live and what you hope to achieve.

The benefits of having a mission statement are profound. It provides direction, acting like a map to guide decisions and actions. It keeps you grounded, and reminds you of your purpose during difficult times. It helps maintain focus on your goal and purpose, and shifts your attention from challenges to opportunities. It aligns you with God's plans, reinforcing faith and values. Most importantly, it encourages continuous growth, pushing you toward greater success and impact.

When you define your mission, you create a foundation that will sustain you through every challenge. No matter what life throws your way, you will always have a clear path forward. In the end, true success isn't just about personal achievement—it's about fulfilling God's purpose, growing in wisdom, and lifting others along the way.

Very Important Next Step

Take five minutes today to start crafting your personal mission statement. Write it down, even if it's not perfect—clarity comes with time, action and reflection. This simple yet powerful exercise will help you define your purpose, stay focused on your goals, and align your actions with your deepest values, especially during difficult times.

A personal mission statement is more than just words; it's a guiding force that keeps you grounded and intentional. As you refine your mission statement, you'll gain a stronger sense of direction, and it'll become easier to prioritize what truly matters and stay resilient through adversity.

To begin, reflect on your core values and purpose. What drives you? What impact do you want to have? Open a notebook or digital document and jot down your thoughts. Focus on three key components: your focus (what you aim to achieve), your purpose (why you're here), and your function (how you will fulfill that purpose). Don't overthink it—just start writing. Revisit and refine it regularly as your goals evolve and new insights emerge.

If you already have a mission statement, use these five minutes to refresh or update it. Life changes, and so does our understanding of purpose. Ensuring that your mission statement remains relevant and inspiring will keep you motivated to move forward. This simple yet intentional step can shape your journey, bringing clarity, fulfillment, and a renewed sense of direction.

Worksheet or Exercise for Growth

1. Write down your Focus, Purpose, and Function.

2. Reflect on Bible verses that inspire you and incorporate them into your mission statement.

3. Place your mission statement in a visible spot and recite it daily.

Your mission statement is a living document. Revisit it regularly and allow it to evolve as you grow and adapt.

Now that you've drafted your mission statement, you're one step closer to living a purposeful and resilient life. In the next chapter, we'll explore how to identify and document your values, the foundation upon which your mission stands.

CHAPTER 21

Decide on Your Values

Why did the value cross the road? To keep the mission on track! Without strong values, even the best plans can veer off course. Staying true to your values keeps you grounded and ensures every step aligns with your purpose, no matter the obstacles.

Values shape who we are and the path we take. Hard work, resilience, and faith carried me through my toughest seasons— from struggling in medical school to juggling multiple jobs. In tough times, it's not luck but deeply rooted values that sustain us.

In this chapter, you will learn the importance of identifying and committing to your core values. Your values define you and shape your decisions, priorities, and actions. They act as a moral compass, helping you navigate life's challenges and stay true to your mission. By the end of this chapter, you'll identify your top values and learn how to align them with your life and mission.

Your values define the legacy you leave, influencing both your achievements and the lives you touch. True fulfillment isn't found in external success alone, but in living with integrity and purpose. As Albert Einstein wisely stated, striving to be a person of value is the greatest pursuit

"Try not to become a man of success, but
rather try to become a man of value."

– Albert Einstein

How This Worked for Successful People: Howard Schultz

Howard Schultz, the visionary former CEO of Starbucks, exemplifies how defining and living by clear values can shape enduring success. Raised in a working-class family in Brooklyn, Schultz watched his father struggle with low-paying jobs that offered no benefits or security. That experience deeply impacted him and became a driving force behind one of his core values: dignity for every worker.

When Schultz joined Starbucks, he wasn't just selling coffee—he was building a company grounded in respect, inclusion, and human connection. He introduced groundbreaking policies like offering comprehensive health insurance to both full- and part-time employees and providing stock options to baristas. These decisions were not based on traditional business metrics but rooted in his values of fairness, loyalty, and community.

Even when facing criticism from shareholders focused on short-term profit, Schultz remained committed to what he believed was right. His value-driven leadership not only cultivated a loyal workforce but also established Starbucks as a purpose-driven brand admired worldwide.

Schultz's story shows that values are not just abstract ideals—they're powerful tools for decision-making, culture-building, and long-term growth. By anchoring his leadership in deeply held principles, he turned a small Seattle coffeehouse into one of the most respected global companies.

My Story

My mission statement has long been my guiding light, shaping the values that define me. Though my values have evolved, their core remains steady, offering clarity, and anchoring me through life's uncertainties. For our years, I have lived by seven values, each a pillar supporting my mission and purpose.

At the foundation of everything is my commitment to putting God first—in my love, time, money, and talents. For more than two decades, I have practiced tithing—giving ten percent of my income to God through my local church, along with additional offerings. Financial challenges have come and gone, but I trust in God's unwavering faithfulness.

My second value is to inspire. I believe in leading by example, showing others that we are all children of a loving Heavenly Father with a purpose for our lives. One way I live this value is by sending daily Bible verses to encourage and uplift others. My current list has grown to 72 people, and I commit to adding three new individuals every month, expanding my reach of encouragement and faith.

Investing is another key principle that guides me—I invest my time, money, and talents into fulfilling my mission and creating a legacy. This means prioritizing meaningful work, making sacrifices for long-term success, and dedicating time to my personal and professional mission. For example, I have devoted countless weekends to teaching and mentoring, even while balancing an intense career.

Being impactful also drives me. I actively seek opportunities to support others, whether through professional mentorship, research guidance, or personal encouragement. I meet with mentees regularly, helping them navigate their paths, just as others once guided me.

Balance is essential for long-term success. I endeavor to nurture my spiritual life, ministry, family, career, health, finances, and relationships, ensuring that I grow in all aspects. Despite my busy schedule, I exercise daily, averaging 12,000 steps and incorporating resistance training to maintain my health and well-being.

Charity is at the heart of how I engage with the world. I strive to love and uplift others, regardless of their circumstances, bringing out the best in them. Whether it's family, friends, colleagues, or patients, I seek to show love in every relationship, ensuring that those around me feel valued and encouraged.

Finally, hard work is a value I first learned from my parents and later deepened through God's Word. The Bible reminds us in 2 Thessalonians 3:11 (AMP), *"Indeed, we hear that some among you are leading an undisciplined and inappropriate life, doing no work at all, but acting like busybodies [meddling in other people's business]."* This scripture underscores the importance of diligence, and I have applied this lesson throughout my life.

My fourth year of medical school was one of my toughest—I failed nearly all my end-of-posting exams. Determined to turn things around, I adopted a rigorous schedule—waking up at one a.m. to study until seven a.m., attending classes and ward rounds from seven a.m. to seven p.m., and sleeping from seven p.m. to one a.m. for an entire year. This commitment to discipline and perseverance helped me overcome the obstacles before me, proving that hard work can transform even the most difficult circumstances.

Financial hardships have also tested my resilience, often forcing me to work multiple jobs. Yet, every challenge reinforced my commitment to creativity, discipline, and persistence. Through these experiences, I have learned that success isn't just about talent or luck—it's about aligning values with daily actions, pushing forward even when the path is uncertain.

Philippians 4:8 (AMP) encourages us to focus on what is true, honorable, and admirable: *"Finally, believers, whatever is true, whatever is honorable and worthy of respect, whatever is right and confirmed by God's word, whatever is pure and wholesome, whatever is lovely and brings peace, whatever is admirable and of good repute; if there is any excellence, if there is anything worthy of praise, think continually on these things [center your mind on them, and implant them in your heart]."* When we center our lives on these principles, we build a foundation that cannot be shaken.

Living by these seven values has given me purpose, stability, and joy.They anchor me, ensuring that no challenge derails my mission. My story is still unfolding, but one thing remains constant—when you align your life with strong values, you are empowered to overcome, grow, and thrive.

Adapt and Advance

Your values form the foundation for who you are becoming, shaping your decisions, actions, and ultimately, your destiny. In the face of challenges, your values keep you steadfast, focusing on what truly matters—your character—rather than fleeting successes or temporary setbacks. Without clear values, it's easy to drift, reacting to life instead of leading it with purpose. But when you anchor yourself in principles that reflect truth, integrity, and faith, you create a guiding force that keeps you aligned with God's purpose, even when trials arise.

Philippians 4:8 (AMP) illustrates this beautifully: *"Finally, believers, whatever is true, whatever is honorable and worthy of respect, whatever is right and confirmed by God's word, whatever is pure and wholesome, whatever is lovely and brings peace, whatever is admirable and of good repute; if there is any excellence, if there is anything worthy of praise, think continually on these things [center your mind on them, and implant them in your heart]."* This verse reminds us that our thoughts shape our values, which in turn guide our actions. By focusing on truth, honor, and love, we align with God's character, and reflect His goodness in our lives.

But how do you uncover and define your values? Start by asking yourself: What principles do I hold dear, even when faced with challenges? What legacy do I want my life to reflect to others? Which traits or actions do I admire most in others? Your answers will reveal the values that matter most to you—the core beliefs that should guide your every decision.

Defining your values brings remarkable clarity and consistency. Decision-making becomes effortless when you measure choices against your core principles, ensuring that your responses to life's highs and lows remain grounded in integrity. As you commit to values-driven living, your character develops, shaping you into the person God created you to be. Purposeful living follows naturally, as each action aligns with a deeper mission, ensuring that your life is not merely spent, but invested in meaningful pursuits.

In uncertainty, when doubt and fear whisper distractions, your values act as a compass, guiding you back to God's purpose. They remind you that resilience is built not on external achievements but on internal conviction. Hold fast to your values, and you won't just navigate life's uncertainties well, but thrive despite them.

Very Important Next Step

Take five minutes today to reflect on the values that shape your character and guide your life. These values are the foundation of your decisions, actions, and the legacy you leave behind. They define you and influence how you navigate challenges, relationships, and opportunities. Identifying and committing to them ensures that you always align with your purpose.

Understanding your values brings clarity, consistency, and strength. When life becomes overwhelming, they anchor you, keeping you steady and focused on what truly matters. They direct your decision-making, helping you stay true to your mission. Without clear values, it's easy to be swayed by fleeting emotions or outside pressures. But, when you know what you stand for, you approach life with greater confidence and intentionality.

To begin, take five minutes to reflect on the principles that matter most with you. Ask yourself: What traits do I admire in others? What do I want my life to reflect? How do I want to be remembered? Write down your top three values and keep them visible—a journal, a vision board, or even a daily phone reminder. Revisiting them regularly will help you stay aligned with your goals and reinforce the kind of person you aspire to be.

Spend these five minutes now to define the values that will shape your journey. Whether it's integrity, perseverance, faith, or kindness, let them guide you. Write them down, live by them, and let them lead you toward a life of meaning, purpose, and fulfillment.

Worksheet or Exercise for Growth

1. Write down your top three values and explain why each one is important to you.

2. Reflect on how these values align with your mission statement.

3. Identify one action you can take daily to live out each value.

Values evolve as you grow and face new challenges. Periodically review yours to ensure they still reflect who you are and where you are going.

Now that you've identified your mission statement and values, it's time to clarify the roles that matter most to you. In the next chapter, we'll discuss how to prioritize these roles to live a balanced and fulfilling life.

CHAPTER 22

Prioritize the Roles That Are Important to You

W hy did the man stop juggling his roles? Because he realized that work-life balance is impossible without priorities! Instead of trying to do everything at once, he focused on what mattered most and found true success..

Have you ever felt stretched thin by trying to do it all or impress everyone? You could lose yourself in the process if you don't take a breather and decide what is truly important to you.

Life pulls us in many directions—work, family, personal growth— but true balance isn't about doing it all; it's about doing what matters most. Prioritizing key roles creates a foundation for purpose and fulfillment. Whether nurturing relationships or pursuing dreams, intentional choices shape our destiny. As Shakespeare said, *"It is not in the stars to hold our destiny but in ourselves."*

In this chapter, you'll identify the roles that matter most to you and take responsibility for them. You'll discover that not all roles carry the same weight; some are deeply connected to your unique purpose in life. By prioritizing these roles, you can live a life of fulfillment, faith, and intentionality.

"You have to decide what your highest priorities are
and have the courage—pleasantly, smilingly, non-
apologetically—to say 'no' to other things. And the way
you do that is by having a bigger 'yes' burning inside."

—**Stephen R. Covey**

How This Worked for Successful People: Stephen Covey

Stephen Covey, author of *The 7 Habits of Highly Effective People*, mastered the art of prioritization. He structured his week around his key roles—husband, father, leader, and learner—ensuring balance and intentionality. His legacy reminds us that true success is not about doing more but about focusing on what is truly important. When we intentionally define our roles and commit to them, we create a life of meaning, stability, and fulfillment.

My Story

Throughout my life, I've had to juggle the demands of education, a rigorous career, and family responsibilities. But, I made a deliberate decision to prioritize my most important role—that of a husband and father. Providing financial, emotional, spiritual, and physical support for my wife and children was never something I wanted to leave to chance. Instead, I created a structured daily routine with my teenage boys—30 minutes each day dedicated to strengthening our relationship, growing in wisdom, and reinforcing our values.

In the evening, we come together for seven intentional activities: reading and discussing a Bible chapter, expressing gratitude, engaging with a self-help book to inspire growth, listening to a sermon and reflecting on its lessons, addressing important personal and family matters, reciting positive "I am" statements for mental resilience, and ending with prayer. These seemingly small but consistent actions have transformed our bond, built resilience in my family, and provided a framework for navigating life's challenges together. Prioritizing this time has not only strengthened our relationship but has also instilled in my children the importance of balance, faith, and lifelong learning.

Like Covey, I've realized that identifying and committing to the roles that matter most is the key to a fulfilling life. True success is not found in the busyness of life but in the intentional choices we make daily to nurture what matters most.

Adapt and Advance

Raising two teenage boys comes with its challenges—differing opinions, communication barriers, and the ongoing task of guiding them toward a strong, purposeful future. However, through our daily commitment to the seven intentional activities mentioned earlier, I have built a framework that fosters growth, deepens our bond, and strengthens our unity. Prioritizing my role as a father has allowed me to nurture their spiritual, emotional, and intellectual development, ensuring they grow into men of character and purpose. This experience has reinforced a crucial lesson: success in any area of life requires identifying and committing to the roles that matter most.

Caring for those entrusted to us extends beyond mere financial provision; it encompasses emotional support, spiritual guidance, and intellectual growth. *1 Timothy 5:8 (AMP) reminds us, "If anyone fails to provide for his own, and especially for those of his own family, he has denied the faith [by disregarding its precepts] and is worse than an unbeliever [who fulfills his obligation in these matters]."*

While this verse directly applies to family, its message extends to all areas of life—true provision means investing time, wisdom, and presence in those who depend on us. Just as a family flourishes when nurtured, workplaces excel when leaders invest in their teams, friendships deepen when met with care, and communities thrive when each person takes responsibility for their role. Prioritizing our responsibilities means showing up fully, offering guidance, and equipping those around us to succeed. Faith is not merely a belief—it is demonstrated the way we act and support those within our sphere of influence.

Shakespeare's words echo this truth: *"It is not in the stars to hold our destiny but in ourselves."* Our lives aren't ruled by fate but by the intentional decisions we make every day. Taking ownership of our roles—whether as a parent, spouse, friend, leader, or learner—empowers us to shape our destiny. The Bible reinforces this in *1 Timothy 5:8*, reminding us that true faith and integrity lie in fulfilling our responsibilities. While family is my central role, your path may look different based on your unique calling. The key is not just to recognize your roles but to embrace them with purpose and action. Success in life is not about doing it all—it's about doing what truly matters and doing it well.

Very Important Next Step

Take a moment today to reflect on the roles that truly define your life. These roles shape your identity, influence your decisions, and determine where your time and energy should be invested. It's easy to get caught up in endless responsibilities, but prioritizing your top three roles ensures you focus on what truly matters. Write them down and consider one small but meaningful action you can take daily to fulfill each role.

Identifying your key roles provides clarity, allowing you to align them with your values and mission. When you intentionally focus on these roles, you bring greater fulfillment and purpose into your life. Whether it's being a dedicated parent, an impactful leader, or a lifelong learner, embracing your roles with intention ensures you live a balanced and meaningful life.

To begin, take five minutes to reflect on the roles that carry the most weight in your journey. These could be related to family, career, faith, or personal growth. Write down your top three roles and make a conscious effort to take one small action daily to honor each role. Keep your list visible as a daily reminder to stay intentional about your priorities, ensuring that your time and energy are directed toward what truly fulfills you.

Worksheet or Exercise for Growth

1. Write down your top seven roles in life.

2. For each role, identify one specific action you can commit to daily.

3. Reflect on how prioritizing these roles aligns with your mission statement and values.

Prioritizing roles doesn't mean doing everything perfectly; it means being intentional about what matters most. Remember, even small, consistent efforts lead to significant impact over time.

Now that you've defined your mission, values, and priority roles, it's time to craft powerful "I am" statements for daily affirmation and growth. These declarations will help you stay aligned with your purpose and build resilience.

CHAPTER 23

The Power of "I Am" Statements

W hy did the self-affirming person bring a ladder to the bar? To raise the bar on themselves every day!

Success begins with how you speak to yourself. Your words shape your mindset, fuel your perseverance, and define your outcomes. I learned this firsthand, climbing from the 10th to the 95th percentile through intentional self-affirmation and unwavering faith. Your words can transform your reality—starting now.

In this chapter, you'll discover the transformative power of daily "I am" statements. These positive affirmations align with your mission, values, and roles, helping you reframe your mindset, build confidence, and achieve your goals. By speaking life into your future, you can shift your perspective and create a foundation for success, even in challenging times.

.Your words shape your reality—your beliefs, actions, and ultimately, your success. By consistently declaring who you are and who you aspire to become, you program your mind to pursue that vision with confidence and determination. As Norman Vincent Peale emphasized, the way you see yourself dictates your path.

"Change your thoughts and you change your world."

"Formulate and stamp indelibly on your mind a mental picture
of yourself as succeeding. Hold this picture tenaciously.
Never permit it to fade. Your mind will seek to develop the
picture. Do not build up obstacles in your imagination."

—Norman Vincent Peale.

How This Worked for Successful People:
Oprah Winfrey

Oprah Winfrey's life is a testament to the power of affirmations.
Growing up in poverty and facing tremendous hardships, she
refused to let her circumstances define her future. She repeatedly
spoke words of possibility and purpose over her life, affirming that
she was destined for greatness. Phrases like, "I am destined to impact
lives," fueled her determination and shaped her future. Today, Oprah
stands as one of the most influential media moguls, philanthropists,
and visionaries of our time. Her success is a testament to the power
of aligning words with vision and purpose—proving that the
declarations we make can shape the course of our lives.

My Story

Daily affirmations have transformed my journey. Over the years, my
"I am" statements have evolved to reflect my growth, aspirations,
and commitment to excellence. My current affirmations include:
*I am Bold, Brilliant, Caring, Dedicated, Excellent, Favored, Fruitful,
Great, Handsome, Healthy, Muscular, Progressive, Rich, Spiritual,
Successful, and Youthful till old age of 84 years (124/84 mmHg; 84
pulse; 84 kg; 4.8 mmol/L FBS).* These declarations are not just words;
they are the foundation of the life I am building.

A defining moment in my journey came during my psychiatry residency in the United States. After an 18-year gap since medical school, adapting to the U.S. educational system while balancing family and training was daunting. Despite my dedication, my first-year exam results placed me in the 10th percentile. Yet, instead of succumbing to frustration, I leaned into my affirmations. Every day, I declared my success, and envisioned myself in the 90th percentile.

With faith, hard work, and strategic preparation, my affirmations became reality. By my second year, I had soared to the 84th percentile. In my third year, I climbed to the 92nd percentile, and by my fourth year, I reached the 95th percentile. This journey reinforced the truth that the words we speak over ourselves have the power to unlock God's promises and propel us toward our highest potential. Whether in overcoming personal setbacks, professional obstacles, or academic challenges, affirmations are more than just motivational phrases—they are declarations of faith that shape the course of our destiny.

Adapt and Advance

Proverbs 18:21 teaches that *"Death and life are in the power of the tongue, and those who love it and indulge it will eat its fruit and bear the consequences of their words."* This verse underscores the immense power our words have in shaping our reality. Our words—whether filled with faith or fear—shape our thoughts, actions, and outcomes. Affirming God's promises allows us to step into His divine plan, while negative speech creates barriers that limit our potential. Our declarations determine the fruit we reap, influencing everything from our confidence to our ability to persevere in adversity.

Joel Osteen exemplifies this principle. After his father's passing, he struggled with self-doubt and uncertainty, but chose to affirm confidence, strength, and divine guidance daily. As he continued to declare God's promises over his life, his mindset shifted, and he stepped boldly into his calling to lead. Today, he leads one of the largest congregations in the world, proving that words of faith can open doors that fear would have kept shut. His book, *I Declare: 31 Promises to Speak Over Your Life*, encourages believers to do the same—to actively speak God's blessings into existence and trust in His plan. His story is a testament to how affirmations, when grounded in faith, transform not only our mindset but also our destiny.

The Bible reminds us that our words hold creative power—just as God spoke the world into existence, we, too, shape our reality through our declarations. *"Death and life are in the power of the tongue."* When we declare success, wisdom, and breakthrough, we align ourselves with God's plan and activate divine possibilities. However, if we speak of doubt, failure, or negativity, we limit our growth and hinder God's blessings.

Norman Vincent Peale, in his teachings on the power of positive thinking, emphasized that visualization combined with affirmations can reshape one's life. The mind responds to the images and words we consistently feed it. When we declare, *"I am strong, I am favored, I am more than a conqueror,"* our actions and mindset follow suit. But if we dwell on limitations and failures, we reinforce those very barriers.

Affirmations are not just feel-good statements; they are declarations of faith that can shape our lives. They remind us that setbacks are setups for comebacks, and that with God, all things are possible. By speaking life over ourselves, we take control of our narrative, strengthen our faith, and activate God's best for our lives.

Very Important Next Step

The words you speak over your life can shape your reality. Each declaration you make reinforces your beliefs, influences your mindset, and ultimately directs your actions. When you affirm your identity and purpose daily, you create a foundation for success, resilience, and unwavering faith in God's promises. Beyond motivation, speaking life over yourself aligns your thoughts and actions with your destiny.

Take a moment today to craft three "I am" statements that align with your mission, values, and roles. These statements should reflect who you aspire to be and what you want to manifest in your life. Perhaps it's "I am a person of wisdom and discernment," "I am a strong and faithful leader," or "I am courageous in the face of challenges." Write them down and say them aloud every morning and evening for the next 30 days. Repetition and belief will rewire your thinking, replacing doubt with confidence and fear with faith.

By affirming these truths, you speak encouragement into your life, and also shape your identity. You will notice a shift in how you approach challenges, how you perceive yourself, and how you walk in your calling. This small but intentional habit can create lasting transformation. Start today—your words hold the key to unlocking the greatness within you.

Worksheet or Exercise for Growth

1. Write down three "I am" statements that reflect your mission, values, and roles.

2. Identify one area of your life where affirmations can help you overcome a challenge.

3. Speak your affirmations daily and journal any progress or breakthroughs over the next 30 days.

Affirmations are most effective when combined with visualization and consistent effort. Remember, the power of life is in your tongue—speak words of faith, hope, and determination daily!

With a mission statement, prioritized roles, and powerful "I am" statements, you are building a strong foundation for success. Now it's time to set short-term and long-term goals that align with your vision and propel you toward your dreams.

CHAPTER 24

Set Long-Term and Short-Term Goals

Why did the goal talk with the to-do list? To make sure they were in sync!

A goal without a plan is just a wish. The difference between those who succeed and those who don't isn't talent—it's strategy. Aligning daily actions with long-term goals turns dreams into reality. This chapter will show you how setting clear, purpose-driven goals creates momentum, fosters discipline, and transforms aspirations into achievements. Whether in faith, career, or personal growth, structured goals ensure that every step you take leads somewhere meaningful.

This chapter will help you set long-term and short-term goals rooted in your mission, values, roles, and "I am" statements. You'll discover practical ways to create goals that inspire you, keep you focused, and move you closer to your dreams. By setting clear, intentional goals, you create a roadmap that directs your daily actions toward meaningful progress.

> "Setting goals is the first step in turning
> the invisible into the visible."
>
> —Tony Robbins

How This Worked for Successful People: Bo Jackson

Bo Jackson didn't succeed by chance, but through meticulous goal setting and relentless effort. He didn't just wake up one day and decide to dominate two professional sports; instead he set incremental goals, mastering one skill at a time. In football, he prioritized speed, agility, and strength, ensuring he could outrun and overpower defenders. In baseball, he focused on refining his swing, perfecting his hand-eye coordination, and sharpening his fielding techniques. Instead of getting overwhelmed by the enormity of his ambition, he broke it down into manageable steps, refining his craft until he was ready to compete at the highest level. His disciplined approach serves as a powerful lesson that success is built through intentional, strategic goal-setting and consistent daily progress.

My Story

Like Bo Jackson, my lifelong commitment to scientific research has guided me through every stage of my career. While my goals have evolved, this dedication has remained constant. I published my first scientific paper in 2009 at the age of 30, and since then, I have set a goal to publish four papers annually for 75 years—totaling 300 lifetime publications. This vision has demanded discipline, persistence, and a structured approach to ensure steady progress despite life's inevitable challenges.

To stay on track, I have embedded writing sessions into my weekly routine, scheduling multiple dedicated time blocks both within and outside of my regular work hours. Some of these sessions are solo, allowing for deep focus, while others involve collaboration with mentors and colleagues. These structured writing sessions ensure continuous progress, helping me balance my research ambitions with the demanding schedule of psychiatry residency.

Collaboration has been a cornerstone of my research journey. At every stage—medical school, PhD, postdoctoral training, and now residency—I have worked closely with mentors who have provided guidance, critical feedback, and invaluable opportunities. Unlike simply moving on after completing a degree or phase, I have nurtured these relationships, allowing me to maintain ongoing collaborations with previous mentors. This approach has opened doors to new research projects, publications, and valuable insights that continue to shape my career. For example, after completing my PhD, I remained engaged with my advisors, which led to continued research and publications. Likewise, my postdoctoral mentors continue to support my academic pursuits, reinforcing the importance of long-term professional relationships. This continuous cycle of mentorship and partnership has significantly contributed to my ability to meet and exceed my publication goals.

Despite the intense workload of psychiatry residency, I have remained committed to my research goals. In three years, I published 12 papers and am currently on course to publish 16 by the time I complete my training—proof that ambitious goals, paired with consistent action, lead to results.

If there is one lesson I have learned, it is that sustained success requires intentionality. Structuring time for focused work, seeking and maintaining valuable mentorship, and committing to long-term goals make even the most ambitious aspirations achievable. You, too, can do this. Whether your goals are academic, professional, or personal, commit to them, break them into manageable steps, and surround yourself with people who support your growth. Success is not just about talent—it's about consistency, strategy, and the willingness to adapt and advance, no matter the obstacles.

Adapt and Advance

Philippians 3:14 reminds us, *"I press on toward the goal to win the [heavenly] prize of the upward call of God in Christ Jesus."* This verse embodies persistence, focus, and unwavering faith in the face of life's challenges. It teaches that with clear, purpose-driven goals, every setback becomes a stepping stone rather than a stumbling block.

Joyce Meyer embodies this truth. Despite her personal struggles, including childhood abuse and financial hardship, she set clear spiritual and professional goals. By committing to teaching God's Word, growing in faith, and expanding her ministry, she pressed forward and transformed countless lives. Like her, when you align your goals with God's purpose, you unlock the potential to overcome adversity and fulfill the destiny He has prepared for you.

My own journey in psychiatry residency further illustrates the power of setting meaningful goals. Faced with the need to balance rigorous clinical duties and a passion for research, I partnered with a colleague experienced in secondary data analysis. We dedicated every Friday evening to collaborative research, a commitment that resulted in four published papers, multiple conference presentations, and several additional projects in progress.

In adapting to new circumstances and leveraging teamwork, I found that clear, well-structured goals provided the direction I needed. As Seneca the Younger wisely said, "If one does not know to which port one is sailing, no wind is favorable." This reminds us of the necessity of clear goals in ensuring every effort counts toward long-term success.

The importance of having a goal—be it spiritual, personal, or professional—cannot be overstated. I use the SMART framework to set goals that are specific, measurable, achievable, relevant, and time-bound. Short-term objectives, like running three miles a week, act as essential stepping stones toward ambitious long-term aspirations, such as completing a marathon in a year. Breaking down big dreams into manageable tasks builds momentum and keeps us focused on what truly matters.

To strengthen our journey, we must ground our goals in spiritual truth. I anchor my path with seven core Bible verses, including Matthew 6:33 ("Seek first the kingdom of God"), Philippians 4:13 ("I can do all things through Christ who strengthens me"), and Jeremiah 29:11 ("God's plans for you are good and filled with hope"). These scriptures remind us that our efforts are supported by a divine plan, ensuring that all things work together for our ultimate good. By integrating faith with clear, purposeful goal-setting, we not only adapt to challenges, but advance toward a future filled with promise, resilience, and transformative success.

Very Important Next Step

Setting goals is not just about planning—it is about intentionally shaping your future and aligning your life with purpose. Without clear goals, even the most ambitious dreams remain distant. Based on your mission, values, roles, and "I am" statements, define at least three long-term and three short-term goals. These will serve as guideposts, keeping you focused and moving forward. To strengthen your commitment, identify three Bible verses to serve as your spiritual foundation, and remind you of God's promises as you press toward your goals.

Setting both long-term and short-term goals ensures that your journey remains purposeful and directed. Long-term goals give you vision, while short-term goals create manageable steps that lead to success. When your goals align with your values, you can make intentional decisions that bring fulfillment rather than distraction. However, it's not just about writing goals down—it's about pairing them with scripture that reinforces your faith and fuels your perseverance. The Word of God provides strength when challenges arise, empowering you to stay committed even in difficult seasons. When your goals are grounded in faith, obstacles become stepping stones, and setbacks become setups for greater breakthroughs.

Take five to ten minutes today to write down three short-term goals and three long-term goals using the SMART framework. Pair each goal with a Bible verse that inspires and strengthens you. Revisit your goals regularly, making small but consistent efforts toward achieving them. Faith without works is dead. Backing your goals with faith positions you to walk boldly in your God-given purpose.

Start today—write down your goals, align them with scripture, and begin taking steps toward a life of intentional growth and success.

Worksheet or Exercise for Growth

1. Write three short-term goals and three long-term goals using the SMART framework.

2. Select three Bible verses that resonate with your goals.

3. Reflect on one small daily action to move closer to each goal.

Goals provide direction, but consistency fuels progress. Remember to review and revise your goals regularly to stay aligned with your purpose. Keep pressing forward, and don't stop until you get there!

With your mission, values, roles, "I am" statements, and goals in place, you're building a strong foundation for success. Now, let's explore the next step: Audacious Faith: Unlocking the Power of Bold, Faith-Filled Prayers.

SECTION 7
PRAYER

This section explores the transformative role of prayer, faith, and worship. Across two impactful chapters, we'll explore the essence of audacious faith, bold prayers, and the path to glory, learn to trust in God's sovereignty and to celebrate His goodness through worship and gratitude.

In chapter 25 entitled "Audacious Faith: Unlocking the Power of Bold, Faith-Filled Prayers," you will learn about faith that goes beyond passive belief and actively aligns with God's will. This faith is not just about asking for what we desire, but also about stepping into action, trusting God to intervene in the seemingly impossible situations of our lives.

Through bold prayers, unwavering faith, and courageous actions, we invite God's miraculous power into our journey, allowing us to break through barriers and experience divine breakthroughs. The chapter highlights inspiring examples, such as Joyce Meyer, whose audacious faith turned a small Bible study into a global ministry. Through this chapter, you'll be encouraged to cultivate bold faith and take concrete steps to demonstrate your trust in God's ability to answer your prayers. As you learn to align your prayers with God's will, you'll witness how audacious faith paves the way for extraordinary results.

In chapter 26 entitled "The Path to Glory," you will discover how worship, gratitude, and celebration form the key practices that move you from mourning to joy, helping you thrive through life's challenges.

The chapter provides insight into the power of gratitude, encouraging you to acknowledge God's blessings daily. It also highlights how celebration fosters joy, inviting God's presence into your life. Through personal testimonies, biblical stories, and practical steps, this chapter reveals how you can access God's glory daily, turning sorrow into joy and strengthening your resilience in the process. Examples like the discipline of King David's worship and the celebration practices of Martin Luther will inspire you to embrace worship as a tool for experiencing God's transformative power.

Through these two chapters, you will come to understand that prayer, faith, and worship are interwoven elements of a faith-driven life that positions you to receive and manifest God's promises. These practices deepen your connection with God, open doors for His miraculous intervention, and lead you into the fullness of His glory. By integrating bold prayers and audacious faith into your daily life and committing to consistent worship and celebration, you can navigate challenges with confidence, knowing that God's power is at work within you.

CHAPTER 25

Audacious Faith: Unlocking the Power of Bold, Faith-Filled Prayers

A man prayed for a $10,000 breakthrough by tomorrow. The next day, he found a lottery flyer, but scoffed, "I need money, not a gamble!"

That night, after dreaming of the numbers 7-14-21, he reluctantly bought a ticket. When he missed the jackpot by one number, he heard, "Faith, yes—but you also need math!"

Life's challenges demand bold faith and practical wisdom. Like the man who discovered that faith alone isn't enough, we must balance dreams with deliberate action. In this chapter, you'll discover how aligning your actions with purpose transforms setbacks into stepping stones. Embrace adaptability, advance your goals, and unlock breakthrough success.

In this chapter, you'll also discover how audacious faith leads to extraordinary breakthroughs. Audacious faith is bold, specific, and active—it goes beyond passive belief to align with God's will and step into action. By persevering, facing fears with faith, and trusting in God's sovereignty, you'll discover how bold prayers unlock the impossible and invite God's miraculous intervention.

Embracing such bold, active faith transforms everyday challenges into opportunities for divine breakthroughs. Corrie Ten Boom's words remind us that true faith unlocks miracles by seeing what others cannot.

> "Faith sees the invisible, believes the unbelievable,
> and receives the impossible."
>
> —Corrie Ten Boom

How This Worked for Successful People: Joyce Meyer

Joyce Meyer's journey is a powerful testament to the transformative power of audacious faith. Overcoming deep personal struggles, she transformed her pain into purpose, launching her ministry with a modest Bible study group. Despite limited resources and public skepticism, she prayed boldly, trusting God to use her hardships for His glory. Not content with a small circle, Joyce took courageous steps to expand her ministry, culminating in the launch of "Enjoying Everyday Life," a TV program that spread her message of hope and resilience to millions around the globe. Her story teaches us that humble beginnings can multiply into extraordinary impact when we trust God's purpose.

My Story

Like Joyce Meyer, my journey has also been shaped by audacious faith. In 2021, eighteen years after graduating from a non-U.S. medical school, I matched into my first-choice psychiatry residency program in South Carolina. Having initially failed Step One and hearing countless stories of rejection for older international graduates, I leaned on God's promises. Miraculously, I secured seven interviews and was matched at my desired program. Both journeys demonstrate that when you trust in God's timing and step out in faith, seemingly impossible doors open.

You, too, can apply these principles in your own life first by setting clear, faith-driven goals that align with your purpose and consistently affirm your identity through prayer and positive declarations. Seek mentors, build supportive communities, and take bold actions that reflect your trust in God's plan. Every step of faith, no matter how daunting, can open new doors and lead to breakthroughs you once thought impossible

Adapt and Advance

When my wife faced a high-risk pregnancy with our twins, I turned to God with specific, faith-filled prayers for life, health, and safe delivery. Despite overwhelming fears, I declared His promises with bold conviction, and today our twin boys are healthy teenagers—a living testimony to the power of audacious prayer in times of crisis. This personal experience taught me that in our most challenging moments, specific prayers can guide us to miraculous interventions.

Mark 11:24 (AMP) reminds us, *"Therefore I tell you, whatever you ask in prayer, believe that you have received it, and it will be yours."* This verse emphasizes that our words and prayers have the power to shape our reality when combined with unwavering belief. Bishop T.D. Jakes exemplifies this principle. In his early ministry, facing severe financial hardship, he prayed for provision with steadfast faith. His persistence transformed obstacles into opportunities, enabling him to build a thriving ministry that continues to impact countless lives. His journey reassures us that when we approach prayer with genuine conviction, divine provision moves from promise to reality.

Faith is not passive; it sees the invisible, believes the unbelievable, and receives the impossible, as Corrie Ten Boom wisely said. T.D. Jakes also reminds us that our progress is limited only by the stretch of our faith, urging us to act boldly in uncharted territories. Billy Graham further reinforces that while prayer is the key to heaven, it is faith that unlocks God's promises.

These lessons also come alive through biblical passages : Mark 11:24 teaches us to believe our requests before they manifest; Hebrews 11:6 affirms that God rewards those who earnestly seek Him; and Joshua's bold prayer for the sun to stand still (Joshua 10:12-13) inspires us to engage in fearless, faith-filled prayer. When we align our prayers and actions with God's will, even the most impossible challenges lead us toward breakthrough.

Very Important Next Step

Identify one bold, audacious prayer aligned with God's will and commit to praying it daily with unwavering faith. Along with your prayer, take one concrete action that demonstrates your trust in God's ability to fulfill that prayer. Audacious faith is not passive; it involves both believing wholeheartedly and stepping out courageously, even when the outcome seems impossible.

When you combine a specific, fervent prayer with decisive action, you actively invite God's intervention, break through barriers and unlock miraculous outcomes. Take five to ten minutes today to reflect on a seemingly insurmountable challenge in your life. Write down one specific prayer, asking God to intervene, and then pinpoint one bold step you can take that shows your trust in His promise. Pray this prayer each day with unwavering conviction, and move forward confidently, knowing that your actions and faith together pave the way for divine breakthroughs.

Worksheet or Exercise for Growth

1. Write down one seemingly impossible situation and pray boldly for God's intervention.

2. Identify one fear that holds you back and write a faith declaration to overcome it.

3. List three faith-driven actions you can take this week to align with your prayers.

Faith is not passive—it's bold, active, and aligned with God's promises. Step out in audacious faith daily, and watch God move in extraordinary ways.

Audacious faith unlocks the impossible by combining bold prayers with bold actions. Trust God's sovereignty, persevere through challenges, and let your faith stretch into new territories. Now, let's explore The Path to Glory and how to navigate your journey with grace and purpose.

CHAPTER 26

The Path to Glory

Why did the worshiper bring a ladder to church? To reach the "high notes" of praise!

In this chapter, you'll discover how heartfelt praise, intentional gratitude, and joyful celebration open the door to truly divine blessings. Let the simplicity of worship and communal joy guide you to a deeper connection with God.

In this chapter, you will learn how worship, gratitude, and celebration can transform your life, moving you from mourning to joy and helping you thrive through every challenge. Through personal testimonies, biblical truths, and actionable steps, we will explore how God's glory can become a daily reality in your life.

When you embrace worship, gratitude, and celebration, your sorrow can transform into a source of strength. As Psalm 30:11 reminds us, God turns mourning into dancing and clothes us with divine joy.

> "He has turned my mourning into dancing; He has taken off my sackcloth and clothed me with joy."
> —Psalm 30:11 (AMP)

How This Worked for Successful People: Martin Luther, Corrie ten Boom, Mother Teresa

Worship is more than a ritual—it is a heart-centered act of thanksgiving that unites our entire being with God. I find inspiration in King David's unabashed devotion when he danced before the Ark of the Covenant, demonstrating a love for God that has inspired countless believers. My mornings mirror that passion as I engage in worship through dancing, aerobic exercises, and heartfelt prayers, aligning my spirit with God's glory.

Martin Luther revolutionized worship by introducing hymns in everyday language, enabling all believers to rejoice in God's grace.

Corrie ten Boom's remarkable example—thanking God for even the fleas in a Nazi concentration camp—teaches us that gratitude can flourish in the harshest circumstances.

Joy, as a fruit of the Spirit, becomes our strength during life's most difficult trials. Mother Teresa, despite serving in the most challenging environments, radiated a joy that inspired others to believe in divine love.

My Story

Every day, I dedicate time to immerse myself in His presence, reminding me that true worship transforms our struggles into gratitude. As you begin your day with prayer and reflection, let your heart sing with praise just as our Creator desires.

I have also experienced transformation brought about by thanksgiving in my life—turning deep sorrow into joyful remembrance after the loss of my parents. Each day, I write down one thing I am grateful for, celebrating even the smallest blessings through singing, dancing, or sharing with loved ones. This act of celebration reminds us that joy is found in recognizing God's goodness, and it helps to mend the wounds of grief with hope.

Through daily worship and study of God's Word, I have found that joy sustains me even in turbulent seasons, filling my heart with hope and courage. I regularly spend a few minutes reflecting on Bible verses about joy, inviting God to refresh my spirit and empower me to face each day with renewed strength.

Praise shifts our focus from personal struggles to God's infinite greatness. Like Paul and Silas, whose voices of praise led to their miraculous deliverance from prison, I have experienced moments of divine clarity and peace when I lift my voice in worship. Taking just five minutes each day to praise God aloud has provided me with profound insights and guidance, turning trials into stepping stones for spiritual growth.

Adapt and Advance

Celebration is the natural outpouring of a grateful heart. Gratitude shifts our focus from what we lack to the abundant provision of our Heavenly Father. Cultivating gratitude not only nurtures a thankful heart but also opens our eyes to the miracles around us, reinforcing our trust in God's unfailing care.

Simplicity in celebration helps us to declutter our minds and focus on God's abundant blessings. St. Francis of Assisi embraced a life of simplicity, finding joy in nature and the everyday wonders of creation. In my own life, simplifying my priorities has allowed me to celebrate God's faithfulness each day, reminding me that true joy lies in recognizing the small yet significant gifts that surround me.

Finally, fellowship and communal joy are essential to our spiritual growth. John Wesley's dynamic group meetings and open-air preaching nurtured a vibrant community of believers who supported each other in faith. At Living Faith Church, the Covenant Hour of Prayer has connected me with a global community, enriching my spiritual journey through collective worship and encouragement. When we gather with others in God's name, we not only strengthen our own faith but also create a network of support that uplifts our entire community.

Together, these practices form a tapestry of worship, celebration, gratitude, joy, praise, simplicity, and fellowship that transforms our lives. They remind us that in every moment of challenge or triumph, God's presence is at work, guiding us to a deeper, more fulfilling relationship with Him.

Very Important Next Step

Take five minutes each day to praise God aloud, thanking Him for who He is. When you vocalize your gratitude, you shift your focus away from your struggles, and toward His unmatched greatness. This daily act of praise opens the door for peace, breakthrough, and a renewed sense of strength, inviting God's presence into every aspect of your life.

Find a quiet moment—whether in the morning or evening—to reflect on God's love, strength, and faithfulness, and let these truths uplift your spirit. As you praise, feel His transformative power guiding you to rise above challenges and embrace a life filled with hope and clarity.

Worksheet or Exercise for Growth

1. Write down three things you are grateful for daily.

2. Spend ten minutes each morning in worship, either through prayer, singing, or reflection.

3. Declutter one area of your life to focus on God's blessings.

4. Join or participate in a worship community this week.

God's glory is not a distant promise—it is a daily reality for those who seek Him. Let this chapter inspire you to live with gratitude, joy, and celebration as you continue to adapt and advance.

Worship, gratitude, and celebration are keys to experiencing God's glory daily. By embracing these practices, you can move from mourning to joy, and thrive through life's challenges. As you reflect on this journey, remember: every step you take brings you closer to fulfilling God's purpose.

CONCLUSION

In conclusion, the chapters on meaning making offer a comprehensive guide to navigating life's challenges with purpose, resilience, and faith. By embracing each step—finding meaning in adversity, defining your "why," transforming your struggles into a message, learning from failure, focusing on your vision, navigating deep waters, and journaling through it all—you will be empowered to rise above every obstacle.

As you move forward, remember that your path is not defined by your past, but by where you choose to go. With the tools and insights provided in these chapters, you will create a life that reflects your true purpose, grounded in faith and sustained by resilience. Keep pressing forward, knowing that every challenge is an opportunity for growth, and each step taken brings you closer to the life you envision.

In the 2nd section, on action, the chapters offer a roadmap for overcoming challenges, cultivating resilience, and transforming your life through intentional actions. From taking bold steps to defying limits, mastering your mindset, and implementing small habits for mental health, you were equipped to face life's difficulties head-on. The journey outlined here emphasizes that transformation is possible—no matter where you start—by embracing faith, commitment, and resilience. As you embark on this journey of growth and progress, trust in your ability to overcome adversity and move toward your highest potential, knowing that each step, no matter how small, is a step toward your future success.

In the 3rd section, on planning, we explored the powerful processes of discovering and aligning with God's plan for your life, structuring your goals with clarity and focus, and embracing obstacles as opportunities for growth. By applying the principles of faith in God's guidance, strategic planning, and resilience in the face of challenges, you will achieve your dreams, and live a life filled with purpose and peace. As you embark on this journey, remember that every step, no matter how small, brings you closer to the fulfillment of your divine calling. Trust in the plan God has set before you, knowing that each action you take with faith will align you further with His purpose for your life.

In the 4th section, on lifelong learning, we examined how both formal and informal learning can significantly contribute to personal growth and success. By engaging with books, pursuing higher education, and embracing self-directed learning, you set yourself up for continued advancement in all areas of your life. The lessons shared in the accompanying chapters encourage you to prioritize lifelong knowledge acquisition, whether through formal schooling or informal channels. As you develop the habit of continuous learning, you open yourself up to greater opportunities, wisdom, and impact.

In the chapters in section 5, on alliance, we see how relationships, when nurtured with gratitude, empathy, and mutual support, become the cornerstone of resilience and personal transformation. By learning to thrive under stress with the help of strong connections and leveraging those connections to give back, we open the door to exponential growth—not only for ourselves but for those around us. Relationships are not just about surviving life's challenges—they are the means by which we thrive, contribute, and build a lasting legacy.

By the end of section 6, mission statement, you will have gained a comprehensive toolkit to live intentionally and purposefully. From drafting your mission statement to deciding on your core values and prioritizing your most important roles, you will be equipped to navigate life with clarity and focus. The power of "I am" statements and goal-setting will further propel you toward success, grounded in your faith and purpose.

Based on section 7, as you explore the journey of audacious faith and the path to glory, you will find that prayer is more than just a request for God's help—it is a declaration of trust, a step of action, and a pathway to miraculous outcomes. Bold, faith-filled prayers open doors to divine intervention, while worship, gratitude, and celebration invite God's glory into your life, turning sorrow into joy. By embracing these practices, you move closer to living a life that is grounded in God's promises and aligned with His purpose. As you continue on this journey, remember that each prayer, act of worship, and expression of gratitude brings you closer to fulfilling God's extraordinary plan for your life.